Edited by GILBERT GUERIN & MARY C. MALE

ADDRESSING
LEARNING
DISABILITIES
AND DIFFICULTIES

How to Reach and Teach Every Student

Second Edition of
I Can Learn: A Handbook
for Parents, Teachers,
and Students

CORWIN PRESS
A SAGE Publications Company
Thousand Oaks, California

For information:

Corwin Press
A Sage Publications Company
2455 Teller Road
Thousand Oaks, California 91320
E-mail: order@corwinpress.com

Sage Publications Ltd.
1 Oliver's Yard
55 City Road
London EC1Y 1SP
United Kingdom

Sage Publications India Pvt. Ltd.
B-42, Panchsheel Enclave
Post Box 4109
New Delhi 110 017 India

Printed in the United States of America.

Library of Congress Cataloging-in-Publication Data

Guerin, Gilbert R.
Addressing learning disabilities and difficulties : how to reach and teach
every student / by Gilbert Guerin and Mary C. Male.
        P. cm.
Includes bibliographical references and index.
ISBN 1-4129-2561-4 (Cloth) — ISBN 1-4129-2562-2 (pbk.)
    1. Learning disabled children—Education—Handbooks, manuals, etc.
I. Male, Mary. II. Title. LC4704.G84 2006
371.9–dc22   2005013305

This book is printed on acid-free paper.

05   06   07   08   09   10   9   8   7   6   5   4   3   2   1

Acquisitions Editor:	Kylee Liegl
Project Editor:	Tracy Alpern
Copy Editor:	Marilyn Power Scott
Proofreader:	Joyce Li
Typesetter:	C&M Digitals (P) Ltd.
Indexer:	Sylvia Coates
Graphic Designer:	Anthony Paular

Contents

Preface

*A*ddressing Learning Disabilities and Difficulties* was first published in
1994 as *I Can Learn: A Handbook for Parents, Teachers, and Students*
with the intention that, while providing guidelines for children and youth
with learning disabilities, it would also be applicable for any student. It
included good teaching practices and an emphasis on the role of the classroom teacher "in creating an environment in which all students could succeed," as the book said. To achieve those ends, the project incorporated the
shared experiences of teachers and, to ensure usefulness, had teachers critique
the manuscript. The book was an overwhelming success.

This revised edition preserves the original intention of the handbook;
provides new information; and updates laws, strategies, and procedures. It is
organized and written to be "friendly" and useful to teachers, parents, and
students. It is designed as a quick reference to critical topics of instruction,
learning, and special education procedures. It reflects changes in law that
resulted from the 2004 amendments to the Individuals with Disabilities
Education Act (IDEA) and reflects developments in effective practices with
children and youth with learning disabilities and learning differences.

Learning problems seldom arrive unannounced, and they have a ten-
dency to generalize across related areas of learning. Problems in learning can
build slowly, and their progression is predictable. For instance, poor reading
skills can result in limited access to the information needed to complete other
assignments, such as writing, discussing, and test taking. As a result, a child
with otherwise good thinking ability can develop a generalized low self-
evaluation because of failures in related areas. Effective strategies can improve
performance and help prevent further failure.

Addressing Learning Disabilities and Difficulties provides useful strategies and promotes procedures to improve student success and to reduce subsequent failure. This book is for those who raise or instruct children or youth
who struggle to learn in school.

Acknowledgments

This book springs from and updates the first edition, titled *I Can Learn: A Handbook for Parents, Teachers, and Students*, which was developed through a contract with the San Jose State University Foundation. The work was conducted by a development team and assisted by an advisory committee representing a broad spectrum of individuals, organizations, and public agencies involved in the education of students who experience learning difficulties in school. Its publication was made possible through the efforts of and legislation authored by then Assemblywoman Jackie Speier.

Development Team

Authors/Consultants:

Barbara Bryant Nolan
Christopher Harris
William Wilson

Consultants:

Michael Spagna
Susan Westaby
Jeff Zettel

Project Director:

Janny Latno-Yamate

Advisory Committee

Diana Berliner
Kay Bodinger
Jeff Braden
Carol Brunett
Nancy Cushen White
Lou Denti

Joan Esposito
Nancy Flynn
Len Garfinkel
Michael Goodman
Dan Graham
Frank Graham-Caso
Gloria Heinemann
Rob Kelley
Bob and Yana Livesay
Mary Male
Shannon O'Hara
John Sanchez
Gary Seaton
Jim Simonds
Kay Stanton
Jim Swanson
Elise Thurau
Robert Verhoogen

Additional Assistance

Yana Livesay
Larry W. Douglass

A series of revisions to the first edition were undertaken to reflect the 1997 changes in regulations in IDEA and to incorporate best practices in serving students who have disabilities. These revisions were not published but added to the evolution of the document.

Development Team

Authors:

Gilbert Guerin
Diana Blackmon

Editor:

Allison Smith

Contributors

Beth Rice
Devena Reed
Patrick McMenamin

This revised edition reflects and respects the contributions of the previous development teams, consultants, advisors, and contributors.

Corwin Press gratefully acknowledges the contributions of the following reviewers:

Rachel Aherns
6th Grade Resource Teacher
Summit Middle School
West Des Moines, IA

Deborah Alexander
Principal
2004 TN Principal of the Year
Kingston Elementary School
Kingston, TN

Pamela Tabor
Elementary Math Specialist
Roye-Williams
   Elementary School
Havre de Grace, MD

Michelle Blakesley
Assistant Principal
Round Rock ISD
Round Rock, TX

Julie Van Den Brandt
K–9 LD Teacher
Appleton Area School District
Appleton, WI

Laura Cumbee
Classroom Teacher
South Central Middle School
Emerson, GA

Linda Reiten
Chairperson and Professor
   of Special Education
University of Montana
   Western Dillon, MT

Colleen Ketcham
Program Manager
EED–Special Education
State of Alaska
   Department of Education
Juneau, AK

About the Editors

 **Gilbert Guerin, PhD**, is on the staff of the San Jose State University Foundation where he directs teacher preparation and demonstration projects. Previously he held the position of professor of special education and department chair at San Jose State University. He has also held faculty positions in the schools of Education at the University of California at Berkeley, in Educational Psychology at California State University, Hayward and in Psychology at Dominican College, San Rafael, California. He was a school psychologist for more than 10 years and holds teaching credentials in elementary education, secondary education, and special education. He is the author of *Informal Assessment in Education; Improving Instruction for Youth at Risk;* and *Critical Steps in Curriculum Reform* and coauthored *Bridges to Reading*. He is the coauthor of recent articles titled "Confronting the Problem of Poor Literacy: Recognition and Action," "Plans, Predictions, and Frustrations in the Education of a Troubled Youth: Michael's Story—One of Many," and "Dropout Prevention: A Case for Enhanced Early Literacy Efforts." He is a mentor and trainer with the Monarch Project, University of Illinois at Chicago, and has provided similar services for the Alliance Project at Vanderbilt University. He has developed an online instructional resource site for high school teachers of students who are at risk for school failure (found at http://alternativeed.sjsu.edu). He actively supports parent participation in the instructional decisions for children and youth and collaborates with Parent Helping Parents, a family resource center.

Mary C. Male, PhD, is a professor of special education at San Jose State University, where she has taught for twenty-two years. She coordinates a federally funded Alternative Education Teacher Preparation Program. Previously, she was a general education classroom teacher in Grades 4, 5, and 6 and a junior high school resource specialist in special education. She has also been a program administrator and staff development consultant for the California Department of Education. She has helped school districts nationwide plan for inclusive classrooms and is an expert in using technology to create access to the general education curriculum. She is the author of *Technology for Inclusion: Meeting the Special Needs of All Students* (2003). Recent book chapters include "Computers and Cooperative Learning in Diverse Classrooms" in *Cooperative Learning and Strategies for Inclusion* by Joanne Putnam (1998) and "Tools for Reconceptualizing the Inclusive Classroom" in *New Ways of Looking at Learning Disabilities* edited by Lou Denti and Patricia Tefft-Cousin (2001). She has presented at conferences nationwide on strategic planning for comprehensive systems of personnel development, cooperative learning, technology and inclusion, and alternative education. She is an Apple Distinguished Educator. She is the parent of a student with disabilities. She is active in her community by serving as a Court-Appointed Special Advocate (CASA) and is a mentor for students in the foster care system who have a dream of a higher education.

1 Introduction

The primary purpose of *Addressing Learning Disabilities and Difficulties: How to Reach and Teach Every Student* is to provide information and suggestions to parents, teachers, and administrators who work with and are concerned about children who have learning and performance problems in school. All children can learn; however, they differ in their abilities to learn, ways of learning, and methods of expressing what they have learned.

This handbook is designed for use as a guide by those who want to help children who have learning difficulties or learning disabilities. It strives to present information in clear and simple language. The content offers strategies that special education teachers, general education teachers, and parents can implement. These strategies can help reduce the frustration of teachers and parents and the failure of students; they can lessen the need for extensive assessment; and they can help children avoid the need for special education placement.

This introductory chapter considers the following subjects:

- Some background of difficulties with children's learning and performance
- Complexity of learning and performance difficulties
- Basic assumptions
- Current approaches to children's difficulties in learning and performance
- Uses, benefits, and limitations of *Addressing Learning Disabilities and Difficulties*
- The overall content and organization of this handbook and tips for using it

SOME BACKGROUND OF DIFFICULTIES WITH CHILDREN'S LEARNING AND PERFORMANCE

For many years, parents and teachers have been concerned about children who seem as though they should be doing better in school. Over the years, thinkers, researchers, and practitioners from education, psychology, and medicine have promoted a variety of explanations for poor achievement. The debates on what constitutes a learning disability continue to add confusion to the general applicability of research findings. The lack of consensus interferes with a clear understanding of conditions, such as, dyslexia, where different evidence seems to support a range of conflicting causes, including poor or inappropriate reading instruction and underlying neurological conditions.

Each new point of view and understanding about learning and behavior tends to give rise to a new procedure to ameliorate children's learning difficulties. A variety of teaching techniques, teaching materials, psychotherapeutic approaches, physical exercises, diets, medications, relaxation treatments, play therapies, art therapies, music therapies, and computer-aided instructions have been developed, prescribed, and tried with children. Children have been taught by college student tutors; by experienced teachers in small, medium, and large classes; and by teachers trained in special techniques of instruction. The effects of the treatments have been mixed. Some children benefited; others did not. Because children have such varied patterns of individual characteristics, it has been difficult to examine the research and come to any definite conclusion about what works across a broad spectrum of learning behaviors. What can a parent and teacher do? How can the child be assisted in learning and performing?

Contemporary research has emphasized the variety of ways in which children receive information, process it, learn it, and apply it. Other research has increased knowledge about effective learning elements and sequences and the strategies of effective learners. Combined, this knowledge has led to an emphasis on instructional approaches that favor identifying *different learning abilities in children* rather than focus on *learning disabilities within children.* Using an abilities approach, observations and interventions are focused on how an individual child works most effectively and what useful skills and strategies can be added to the child's repertory. In this way, instruction can be built around how an individual approaches, perceives, and acts on a skill and the interventions that can enhance learning.

Observation can build a collective understanding of a child's performance. Information gathered by parents and teachers can increase understanding about how a child plays and learns—when alone, in a small group, in a classroom, on the playground, on a school bus, at home, and in the neighborhood. What skills does the child demonstrate and in what settings? Which activities does the child enjoy and seek out and which are avoided? These observations provide opportunities to develop a well-rounded picture of the child based on observations by persons most familiar with the child's behavior.

Observation is aimed at recognizing ineffective learning or voids in learning before they lead to habitual inaccuracies or generalize into other behaviors. Early observation and intervention is aimed at finding out *how and what* a child learns and *how and what* learning a child can demonstrate toward specific learning goals and standards. When a child's learning and performance is periodically measured and monitored, the teacher can determine the effectiveness of instruction and make changes. When this information is open to the child and the parent, they have information upon which to set personal goals and to judge the effectiveness of their efforts. In this context learning can become a collaborative adventure.

COMPLEXITY OF LEARNING AND PERFORMANCE DIFFICULTIES

Assessing the difference between academic underachievement and a learning disability or an attention deficit problem is difficult. Furthermore, it must be acknowledged that without expert assistance, teachers and parents cannot help all students, no matter how hard they (and the children) try. Some students do not seem to benefit from adaptations in general classroom instruction. These children may be referred for assessment. If a child is identified as having exceptional needs, he or she receives special education services to help overcome the effects of the disability. Terms commonly used to describe some of the learning disabilities are

- Dyslexia
- Developmental aphasia
- Attention deficit disorder
- Attention deficit/hyperactivity disorder

The terms refer *not* to children but to a group or constellation of conditions. At times, the conditions occur in conjunction with other conditions, such as behavioral disorders, emotional disorders, or other health impairments in such combinations as to make them difficult to untangle.

Some students who struggle with class work, who do not seem to benefit from instructional adaptations, and who are referred for assessment may be determined to be ineligible for special education services. But even though these students are not eligible for special assistance, their teachers may be able to use the results of assessment and the accompanying recommendations to make useful changes in classroom instruction.

General education classrooms have always had students with a broad range of learning styles and behaviors, and teachers are accustomed to a variety of learning styles and skills. However, the changing school population, which contains students with an increasing diversity of backgrounds, languages, and cultures, poses additional challenges to educators. The Individuals with Disabilities Education Act requires that students are educated in the least restrictive environment and this increases the variability within classrooms. Current trends foster teaching approaches that recognize and honor a wide variety of cultural and learning differences.

The No Child Left Behind law has mandated that all children are to be served by highly qualified teachers, an achievement that should improve all instruction. A shortage of qualified special education teachers has had a negative impact on special instruction as it has in other areas of instruction. Improvement in the quality of teaching should reduce learning problems that have resulted from poor instruction and poor class management. As knowledge about learning and behavior improves, so will the skills of teachers and parents who are called upon to help children who continue to struggle with learning.

BASIC ASSUMPTIONS

The material presented in *Addressing Learning Disabilities and Difficulties* is based on the following four assumptions:

1. All children want to learn.

2. Most misbehavior or poor academic performance is neither willful nor malicious.

3. Teachers want to teach effectively.

4. Parents want to understand and to support their children's learning.

The following five items are generally accepted concepts regarding the instruction of children:

1. No single general reading or instructional program meets the needs of all students.

2. Some students require additional instruction in reading, writing, and spelling to learn those basic skills.

3. Early identification of learning problems can reduce early school failure, loss of self-esteem, and persistent patterns of difficulty.

4. The middle school years are a time of critical change in the manner of instruction, the learning environment, and adolescent behavior.

5. Reasonable accommodations, as required by the Americans with Disabilities Act (ADA), increase the chances that children who have difficulties will learn.

APPROACHES TO CHILDREN'S DIFFICULTIES IN LEARNING AND PERFORMANCE

Several labels, such as *learning disabled, neurologically handicapped, brain-injured, hyperactive, attention deficit,* or *learning disordered,* have been applied to children who perform poorly in school. Recently, the emphasis has shifted away from applying labels to understanding the variety of ways in which children receive information, process that information, and demonstrate that they have learned and can apply the information. This approach has been termed a *learning abilities* or *learning styles* approach in contrast to a *learning disability* approach.

School professionals who specialize in learning disabilities often use a learning abilities approach or a learning styles approach to education, and they encourage teachers, parents, and students to view learning problems from this point of view. The current approach also stresses early identification of the learning problem and early intervention. When learning problems are identified early in a student's academic career and classroom interventions begin immediately, failure can be averted before it becomes chronic, cloaked in frustration, and destructive to a student's self-esteem and motivation. Children who experience more successes than failures in school develop the confidence and persistence that lead to increased learning.

The identification of learning strengths and weaknesses in a student or a group of children can lead to the use of instructional strategies that are tailored toward individual needs. Information about learning strengths and weaknesses can provide parents with an understanding of the ways in which their child learns and the ways in which they can help their child at home. Individualized information can also provide a child with better self-understanding and help that child recognize personally effective learning strategies.

One important feature of effective instruction is the documentation of strategies that benefit a child's learning and behavior. Another feature is the maintenance of a record of a student's plans, accomplishments, and evaluations. Teachers save samples of a student's work, evaluations, and achievements. Parents can keep a folder that contains records of their child's learning needs, a history of the child's progress, and copies of his or her schoolwork. In many classes, students keep portfolios of their work so that they can demonstrate their proficiency and track the effect of changes in their study strategies. Such documentation of interventions and progress provides a basis for future plans.

Scientific, medical, and educational researchers are making steady progress in understanding the ways in which children and adults learn. Readers who want more information about specific learning difficulties or disabilities or about the latest research regarding multiple learning styles are encouraged to look into the professional literature in a school or public library. Information can also be obtained by speaking personally with knowledgeable professionals in the field and by searching the Internet site of the center or association dedicated to the disorder. The appendices of this handbook also provide useful information.

USES, BENEFITS, AND LIMITATIONS OF *ADDRESSING LEARNING DISABILITIES AND DIFFICULTIES*

Parents and educators can use this handbook to assist students who experience learning or behavioral difficulties in school. Because students do not learn or demonstrate what they have learned in the same ways, having a variety of teaching strategies and methods provides all students with opportunities to learn.

Uses

This handbook is designed to

1. Help parents and educators improve their understanding of the needs and the behaviors of students who have problems in learning or in school performance, including children who have learning disabilities, such as dyslexia, attention deficit disorder, and attention-deficit/ hyperactivity disorder

2. Promote effective instructional techniques for use with all children but especially for use with students who have problems in learning or performance

3. Provide references for information and resources that can assist parents, teachers, and administrators in improving the effectiveness of instruction and educational programs

4. Provide information on characteristic behaviors that can be used as a basis for screening students for difficulties in learning and in performance

5. Provide pertinent citations for the federal laws and regulations that apply to referral for assessment, determination of eligibility, and provision of special education and related services to children who have specific learning disabilities

6. Provide information about school practices that help all students succeed

Benefits

The information in this handbook and its application are intended to help provide a variety of benefits and positive outcomes for the following groups:

Students

Students will find that some of the information provided in this handbook refers to the learning situations that they experience in their classrooms. Students should think of the learning strategies provided in this text as possible avenues for self-help. When students believe that certain suggestions might help them learn, they should discuss these suggestions with their teachers or parents. Strategies might not be adopted exactly as they are presented in this guide because the strategies need to fit individual teaching and learning styles. In addition, a trial-and-error period often needs to take place before a successful strategy is discovered. The old adage "try, try again" represents a helpful attitude for both students and teachers. A learning difficulty or disability usually appears slowly over time, and solutions can be equally slow in developing.

Teachers

This handbook provides information about the characteristics of learning difficulties and disabilities. It provides descriptions of learning difficulties and suggests teaching strategies that relate to specific classroom skills and tasks. Because each teacher has his or her own interests, teaching style, and classroom situations, the intention of this handbook is to provide a variety of teaching strategies from which teachers can select the ones that best fit them and their students. The suggestions that appear in this text represent a starting point, and teachers will likely want to combine, modify, and otherwise adapt strategies to specific classroom needs.

Parents

Parents can use this handbook along with their existing knowledge of their child's learning styles, behaviors, and feelings about school to assist their child at home and in working with school staff. It can be tempting to identify all the difficulties that a child exhibits and to overlook his or her areas of strength or the areas in which the child has no problems. To counterbalance these tendencies, parents can use the lists of strategies that are provided in Chapters 2 and 3 to discover and to highlight the areas in which no problems exist and the areas in which their child's strengths can be used to improve learning. For example, a child who has good attentional and listening skills but poor reading skills can be helped to process information by listening to others read or by using audiotapes. A child who has good thinking skills but poor attentional skills might learn best by doing projects rather than by attempting paper-and-pencil tasks. Parents are often more aware of their child's interests and aptitudes than are school professionals. Parents can use their knowledge of their child's strengths and interests when they help their child with homework, and they can often help their child's teacher in discovering effective teaching avenues.

School Districts and School Leaders

This handbook can be used as a part of staff development programs for general education teachers and for other school personnel. It can be used to stimulate thoughtful, professional conversations about the ways in which a school and its faculty and staff can assist all students in succeeding in school. This handbook can also be used as a reference guide to help teachers and other school personnel understand individual students who have academic difficulties, apply successful interventions, and make appropriate referrals for further evaluation.

Administrators, consultants, supervisors, other professionals, and board members often face making decisions that affect unsuccessful students. This handbook can provide an understanding of the complexities encountered by teachers and parents who work to improve students' performances. This publication also provides information about the instructional steps that can help reduce a student's academic problems and improve his or her learning. In addition, it describes ways to organize instructional programs to meet the educational needs of students who are experiencing difficulties. Most of these students can be served exclusively by general education; however, some students will need additional support in the form of related services or special education.

Limitations

The strategies in this handbook are intended for use as procedures and tools that can assist teachers, parents, and administrators in effectively instructing all children and especially those children who fail to learn with standard group instruction. They have been drawn from the collective experience of many professionals and parents who have worked with students who have learning difficulties. Although it is comprehensive, *Addressing Learning Disabilities and Difficulties* does not include all available strategies nor does it include complete instructional programs that might be helpful to teachers, parents, and students. No single strategy will suit the unique abilities and disabilities of all learners. Nor is there a particular service delivery model that will suit the particular assets and challenges of each school site. Because students have unique combinations of strengths, weaknesses, needs, and interests, different strategies may have to be tried before an appropriate intervention is found. If difficulties persist after parents and teachers have collaborated and after a school-level team of teachers and other education professionals have met and provided suggestions for modifying instruction or the student's behavior, then a formal, professional assessment may be needed. Some learning problems defy the best classroom strategies. No matter how hard a child, parent, or teacher may work on a problem, a student's failure to learn may continue. Even when a child who is formally tested does not meet eligibility criteria for receiving special education services, information gained through a formal assessment can provide suggestions for classroom instruction and home assistance. An effective assessment team can not only determine eligibility but can also identify a child's learning strengths and weaknesses. The team can determine potentially effective teaching strategies and can recommend other forms of assistance.

PARTS I AND II: THEIR CONTENT AND PURPOSE

The main body of the handbook is divided into two sections. Part I, "Learning Difficulties and Teaching Strategies," examines the characteristics of children who have general learning difficulties; the difficulties and strategies related to learning skills; and the difficulties and strategies related to performance skills. Part II contains a chapter on referring students to special education and the eligibility of students who have learning disabilities. It also examines the individualized education program (IEP) process and the options for service delivery.

The purpose of Part I is to

1. promote knowledge of classroom strategies that have been used successfully with children who have difficulty learning,

2. enable special and general education teachers to select strategies that are appropriate to the needs of specific students and to adjust teaching styles to classroom situations,

3. provide an understanding of the difficulties and strategies related to learning skills and performance skills.

The purpose of Part II is to

1. clarify the process of referral, assessment, eligibility, and parental involvement and

2. help parents and educators understand the IEP process, service delivery options, and the role of the school site.

The three resources at the end of this handbook provide the following information:

Resource A: A brief discussion of the characteristics of learning disabilities, dyslexia, attention disorders, and behavior problems

Resource B: Addresses to selected Internet sites for readers who want additional information about the topics examined in *Addressing Learning Disabilities and Difficulties*

Resource C: A list of public agencies, foundations, centers, parent organizations, and state and national professional organizations through which help may be obtained for persons who have learning disabilities in their families

In addition, a glossary of terms that appear in this handbook, in federal and state laws, and in regulations has been included along with a section on selected references for further reading.

WAYS TO USE THIS HANDBOOK

Addressing Learning Disabilities and Difficulties is meant to assist professionals and parents who are interested in the instruction of children who have learning difficulties and learning disabilities. It can be opened at any section and used to facilitate understanding and instruction; however, to gain a full appreciation of learning difficulties and disabilities, professionals and parents should read this handbook in its entirety. (Readers may wish to refer to the glossary if they encounter a term with which they are unfamiliar.)

The following sequence suggests a method for using *Addressing Learning Disabilities and Difficulties* to move from the recognition of a problem to the application of a strategy:

1. Record observations of a student's learning and performance strengths and weaknesses.

2. Select and employ the strategies suggested in the sections of Chapter 1 titled "Characteristics of Learning and Performance Difficulties" and "Accommodations and Modifications" to improve students' general learning or performance skills.

3. Determine the areas of a student's learning or performance skills to be improved by using in-class observations. Read the pertinent sections in Chapters 2 or 3 and select appropriate strategies of instruction.

4. Work with one of the student's learning or performance skills and record the results of the actions that you have taken.

5. Record the strategies as you use them.

6. Discard the actions that do not produce results after a reasonable trial period. Start again with Step 2 and repeat the process until success is achieved.

The formatting in Chapters 2 and 3—which contain descriptions of characteristics typically seen in students who have learning difficulties and suggested strategies for teaching these students—allows the reader to reproduce pages that relate to a single instructional topic. In this way, specific information can be inserted into a class planning book or among homework references. The topics can be used for professional discussions, as planning aids by a teacher and a parent, as a focal point for teacher collaboration, or as material for staff development activities.

An Intervention Plan work sheet is provided at the end of each chapter that contains teaching strategies. The work sheet may be reproduced and is designed to assist the reader in matching strategies with instructional objectives and in selecting strategies that could be used with an entire class or that are appropriate for an individual child.

In this handbook, references are made frequently to federal laws and regulations. In the case of IDEA 2004, for which regulations have not yet been formulated, the law itself is referenced. Until those regulations are formulated and approved, regulations from IDEA 1997 are in effect. Examples of original citations and the abbreviated forms of citations used within the text appear as follows:

- *Code of Federal Regulations, Title 34,* Section 300.7(c)(10), revised as of July 1, 2000, is reported as 34 *CFR* 300.7(c)(10).

SUMMARY

This handbook provides information about learning difficulties that educators and parents encounter in general education classrooms, special education programs, or in the home. The strategies that are presented in Part I of this handbook are based on the underlying assumptions that children want to learn and can learn and that teachers and parents want to help. This handbook can assist special education teachers and general education teachers, parents, and other education professionals in their search for effective instructional strategies. Children whose problems persist in a general education setting after team efforts and attempts at interventions have been made should be considered for referral to special education. The process of referral, the determination of eligibility, and the delivery of services are the core topics of Part II of this handbook. The intention of *Addressing Learning Disabilities and Difficulties* is to give teachers and parents the tools that they need to provide students with improved instructional and behavioral services.

PART I

Learning Difficulties and Teaching Strategies

2 Strategies to Improve Learning Skills

Ginny is a fourth grade student in Mrs. Grace's class. She is a very enthusiastic learner who has difficulty sitting still during direct instruction time. She doodles while Mrs. Grace is talking, which makes Mrs. Grace think she isn't paying attention. Her backpack has dozens of papers scrunched in the bottom, and her grades show a number of assignments that were not turned in. Her poor grades are a concern to her parents, and her teacher wants to help.

This chapter describes the skills that students need to be efficient learners. These skills are listening comprehension, ability to pay attention, organizational skills, retention and retrieval of material, productivity, mathematical computations and operations, mathematical reasoning and problem solving, reading word recognition, and reading comprehension. The discussion of each skill consists of a list of common difficulties and a list of suggested strategies for improving the skill.

In general, the skills that are discussed in this chapter are the "getting ready to learn" skills and the basic academic skills, and it begins with a discussion about the skill of listening, a key element in the learning process. Closely linked to the skill of listening is the ability to pay attention, the second topic that is considered in this chapter. A student must be able to listen to instruction, pay attention long enough to receive the instruction, and hold a focus during practice and mastery. Each skill is an interdependent part of the learning process. Failure in one part will reduce a student's ability to receive, retain, or demonstrate knowledge or skill.

Three often-seen characteristics of students who have learning difficulties are poor organizational skills, poor memory skills, and reduced productivity. This cluster of skill deficiencies clearly signals the need to increase assistance. It is possible that a student's ability to organize, to memorize, and to be productive will improve as the student becomes a more effective learner in an academic area, such as in reading comprehension. However, it is also likely that strategies discussed under these topics can help to frame the way instruction is provided in an academic area and can support general instruction.

Mathematics is a fundamental content area that requires basic skills. It is a process in which each step tends to depend on the acquisition of earlier math skills: Failure to learn a basic element can interfere with subsequent learning. Math is also a basic skill that is used in other subject areas, such as science. Science as a content area depends heavily on both reading and mathematics skills.

The ability to read is the single most necessary academic skill for achieving success in school. Reading becomes more important at each successive grade level because it is critically important for gaining access to information, understanding directions, reviewing written notes, and grasping word problems. For each of these activities, effective accommodations exist to help poor readers, but effective use of these accommodations often relies on the willingness and skill of the teacher.

Both reading and mathematics have learning and performance components. For example, reading in the primary grades is often done orally as practice and as a demonstration of word decoding and reading fluency. Computation in math is generally seen as a performance skill. For easy reference, this guide covers all the components of mathematics and reading in this chapter.

LISTENING COMPREHENSION

Listening is a skill that is frequently required of students both at home and in school. In many classrooms, students spend more time listening than speaking, reading, or writing. Adults often believe that a student is purposefully inattentive when in fact the student has not fully understood a spoken statement or has been unable to remain focused on a long, spoken presentation.

Difficulties

Students who have difficulties processing, attending to, or understanding verbal instruction typically

1. Appear to lose interest or become inattentive during oral presentations.

2. Seem to daydream or to become restless when listening is required.

3. Have difficulty remembering things that are told to them.

4. Have difficulty following spoken, sequenced directions.

5. Ask the teacher or a classmate to repeat directions or facts just presented.

6. Look to see what others are doing immediately after multistep directions have been given.

7. Give answers that seem unrelated to the questions.

8. Appear to be distracted easily by background noise.

9. Appear unable to listen and to write notes simultaneously.

Strategies

Table 2.1 lists strategies to facilitate a student's listening comprehension.

ABILITY TO PAY ATTENTION

Students who have learning difficulties can have special problems with paying attention. Attentional problems consist of the difficulty that some students have in working for extended periods of time or the trouble that they have focusing on a subject or an activity for even a short period of time. Activities that a student enjoys tend to hold the student's attention better than activities that the student does not enjoy. The need for deliberate or purposeful attention is greatest when the student is learning a new process; once learned, the mechanics of a task, like reading, become partly automatic and require little attention. Students who have learning difficulties often find little enjoyment in their struggles to learn, particularly when the processes that have become automatic for average learners still require an unreasonable amount of their attention. For this reason, inattention can be an expected contributor to school failure.

Several factors help differentiate expected and age-related problems with inattention and hyperactivity that are attributable to a student's individual temperament from those problems that pose significant interference to learning. Inattention and hyperactivity are assessed on a continuum from mild to severe, depending on their frequency, duration, history, and resistance to change. Attention deficit disorder and attention-deficit/hyperactivity disorder,

Table 2.1   Teaching Strategies to Promote Listening Comprehension and
Ability to Pay Attention

Elem	Mid	Sec	Strategies
X	X	X	Seat the student so that he or she can clearly hear and see the teacher. Avoid seating the student near distracting sounds and sights, such as a heater, fish tank, door, or window.
X	X	X	Make eye contact with the student before you speak and make introductory statements, such as "Really pay attention; this is important," when you are about to deliver important spoken information.
X	X		Keep oral directions simple by using familiar vocabulary and by controlling the rate of delivery. Present directions one step at a time.
X	X	X	Ask the student to repeat or to paraphrase the directions or instructions to verify comprehension.
X	X	X	Select a student who consistently writes complete and legible notes to act as a note taker. Make the notes available to all the students. Rotate this job among students in the class. Discuss and practice the process of note taking.
X	X	X	Use a specific and consistent structure when giving assignments. For example, you might give homework assignments at the beginning of class, write assignments in the upper right-hand corner of the board, and provide time for students to copy and clarify assignments.
X	X	X	Use multiple modalities (seeing, hearing, writing) when presenting new concepts, information, or activities. Ensure that visual aids are clearly visible to all students in the class.
X	X	X	Augment a presentation by using visual props, aids, and gestures. Supplement lectures with audiovisual presentations and hands-on activities.
X	X	X	Write key terms and concepts on the board as you introduce them in your presentation or as they are introduced in the text.
X	X	X	Vary the rate, volume, and pitch of your speech and speak slowly to be understood and to maintain the students' attention.
X	X	X	Interject independent, quiet, visual-motor activities periodically during your presentation to provide students with a respite from listening.
X	X	X	Allow study partners to verbally review directions to verify consistent and accurate understanding of the directions before beginning independent activities.
X	X	X	Accept nondistracting, small motor activities, such as doodling, during listening periods. Understand that some students constructively channel physical energy in this way.

severe forms of attention difficulties that are eligible for special education assistance, are described in Chapter 4.

Difficulties

Students who have problems with inattention or hyperactivity typically

1. Appear to not listen, to daydream, to look around, or to be "blank" or they stare or are distracted by things that no one else notices.

2. Become distracted easily, stop working on a task, or start another task, particularly during activities that they have determined are not interesting, highly stimulating, or enjoyable.

3. Have difficulty concentrating on schoolwork, on tasks that require sustained or prolonged attention, or on activities that occur in large groups.

4. Perform inconsistently or unpredictably and without reasonable explanation, make careless mistakes, and lack persistence.

5. Demonstrate an understanding of the main idea but miss important details.

6. Have difficulty prioritizing the importance of the material presented or attend too much or too long to minor, less important, or irrelevant information.

7. Rush through work, chores, or activities or give up quickly.

8. Become bored or restless easily, shift excessively from one activity to another, are difficult to satisfy, want things right away, think about what is coming next or later, and fail to finish activities.

9. Appear not to plan or to organize before taking action or starting to work.

10. Act or speak out quickly or carelessly and without thinking about consequences.

11. Blurt out answers impulsively, interrupt conversations or presentations with comments that have little or no connection with what is being said or done, and have difficulty waiting for their turn in group activities or games.

12. Have excess energy, are always moving, have difficulty sitting still or remaining in their seats, and fidget excessively.

13. Exhibit variable and unpredictable behavior, make trouble, stir things up without meaning to get into trouble, and annoy or bother others.

14. Have difficulty realizing that they are disturbing others or have difficulty understanding why they have trouble getting along with peers.

15. Have problems recognizing their own or others' mistakes, learning from experience, or improving their conduct after being disciplined or corrected.

Strategies

Students who have problems with inattention or hyperactivity often need changes made to their learning environment. Issues of classroom management emerge as a primary consideration, and strategies that reinforce positive behaviors can be helpful. Strategies to manage students' inattention, hyperactivity, and impassivity are provided in Table 2.2.

ORGANIZATIONAL SKILLS

Organizational problems are clustered into four categories: space, priorities, time, and transitions. Students of different ages who have learning difficulties face different organizational challenges within the four categories. Initially a student may not grasp strategies for organizing his or her world to support classroom learning. As a student grows older, the organizational strategies that most students have assimilated are no longer taught or reinforced in the classroom. As a result, older students who have learning difficulties may need to be reintroduced to these skills.

Difficulties

1. Students who have difficulties in spatial organization typically
   a. Demonstrate poor organization of work on paper, especially when doing mathematical computations or taking notes.
   b. Misplace or constantly forget their homework, pencils, books, and other class materials.
   c. Create messy and disorganized notebooks, assignments, desks, rooms, or lockers.

Table 2.2   Teaching Strategies to Increase Student Attention

Elem	Mid	Sec	Strategies
X	X	X	Decrease the length of assignments or tasks or break assignments into parts that are given at different times, and give fewer problems in all affected subjects.
X	X		Keep directions and rules short and clear. Provide clear procedures for transition periods.
X	X	X	Alternate activities of low interest and high interest. Vary activities during class periods that occur late in the day or that are long.
X	X		Observe carefully a student's behavior to identify particular types of tasks, kinds of activities, or times of day when the student's inattention or hyperactivity occurs or is absent. Record observations and plan interventions.
X			Prepare students well in advance for any changes in their daily classroom routine to eliminate surprises whenever possible and remind the students of these changes and reassure them often.
X	X	X	Shorten teacher presentation time and independent work periods. Include both kinds of activities during class periods to provide respite.
X	X		Develop activities that enable students to leave their seats during controlled activities. Incorporate short periods of physical activity, which may alleviate restlessness and help reduce the onset of distracting behaviors.
X			Provide screened-off carrels or stand-up desks for independent work times or allow students to move to a quiet area in the room.
X	X	X	Establish a secret signal with the student (e.g., a pat on the shoulder) to indicate that you believe that the student is off task. The signal should change gradually from a physical touch to a signal given in proximity to the student, and finally to a subtle cue given from the regular teaching position.
X	X		Encourage students to stop by your desk on their way out of class if they think that they might have missed something important during the lesson. Help students identify specifically the part of the instructions in the lesson that they missed.
X	X	X	Avoid blaming or disciplining students during the discussion.

(Continued)

Table 2.2 (Continued)

Elem	Mid	Sec	Strategies
X	X	X	State clearly your expectations for students' behavior and establish corresponding consequences for specific violations.
X	X	X	Develop a reward-based contract system that also contains clearly understood, progressive consequences for targeted misbehaviors.
X	X		Consider the use of behavior charts and rewards that focus the student's attention on two or three of his or her most distracting behaviors. Rather than emphasize "not doing," reward the student for "doing" correct or desired behaviors.
X	X		Stipulate the minimum time necessary if a time-out from an activity is required. Provide incentives for the student to rejoin the class.
X	X	X	Consider playing soft music in the background during independent work activities. Allow students to stand when they have finished their work or have an easy assignment available to them to complete while they wait for your help.

2. Students who have difficulties organizing priorities typically
   a. Experience difficulty getting started on assignments.
   b. Experience difficulty making choices and identifying priorities.
   c. Become distracted easily by extraneous stimuli and are often deterred from working on tasks.

3. Students who have difficulties organizing their time typically
   a. Lose track of time and always seem to do things at the last minute.
   b. Experience difficulty recalling when and where an event, assignment, activity, and appointment will occur.
   c. Put things off until the last minute and then become panicky.

4. Students who have difficulties making transitions typically
   a. Do not know how to begin or how to end an assignment or activity.
   b. Become disoriented and have difficulty adjusting to changes in routine.
   c. Have difficulty settling down and becoming focused after making a transition from one activity to another.

Strategies

Table 2.3 provides strategies to facilitate students' abilities to organize.

Table 2.3   Teaching Strategies for Organizational Skills

Elem	Mid	Sec	Strategies
X	X	X	Establish and adhere to a daily routine in your classroom and post a daily schedule in either written or pictorial form.
X	X	X	Post and use organizational aids, such as calendars and schedules.
X	X	X	Begin each study unit with a discussion and a calendar that outlines progress points and due dates for all work assigned.
	X	X	Provide students with a study guide that emphasizes important terms and questions that focus on the concepts that you want the students to remember.
X	X	X	Develop with the students a checklist of materials needed or important times and due dates to remember. Review this checklist regularly with the students.
X	X	X	Develop a personalized What I Need to Remember page for each student that highlights three to five of the most important things you want the student to remember routinely. This sheet should be displayed in the student's folder or binder.
X	X	X	Begin each class period with a review of the key points from your last class. End each class period by asking students to summarize that day's lesson.
X	X		Provide students with an outline of the subject to be covered or jointly develop a graphic organizer to demonstrate the relationship between ideas, activities, or information.
	X	X	Assist students in developing a method of note taking that works best for them. Share strategies and periodically review the note-taking methods being used.
X	X		Require students, with each change of activity, to clear their desks of all unnecessary materials and books that might be distracting.
X	X		Set aside a regular time each week during which students clean out their desks and reorganize their binders.
	X	X	Insist that the students carry a binder (or an acceptable substitute) that has sections for each class, including sections for homework assignments and current homework.
X	X		Provide the students with only the pages and the instructions that they will need to do the current assignment when using a workbook.

(Continued)

Table 2.3 (Continued)

Elem	Mid	Sec	Strategies
	X		Have the students periodically check the teacher's master list of in-class and homework assignments and the dates they are due.
X	X		At the top of practice work sheets, provide a model that demonstrates the sequence of steps to successful problem solving. Eliminate problems that do not fit the model.
X	X		Provide a guide for structuring writing assignments, such as a work sheet that requires the student to develop ideas in response to specific topics (e.g., main character, personality trait, or setting).
X	X		Begin a writing assignment by having students record or orally contribute words or concepts that they believe are relevant to the assigned topic. Place these words in a word bank from which students can draw. Younger students may benefit from drawing pictures of their ideas first. Older students may record their thoughts by using a tape recorder so that they do not forget their ideas as they work through the actual writing process.

RETENTION AND RETRIEVAL OF MATERIAL

All of us have had the experience of hearing and understanding a piece of information but not holding it in memory. We have also had the experience of knowing something but being unable to recall it when we needed it. Some students have these two experiences routinely. They have chronic difficulties memorizing information or recalling it, and these difficulties have a significant impact on learning. Good short-term memory skills most often account for the greatest difference between average students and students who have learning difficulties.

Sandra is a student in Ms. Long's American literature class. She has no problem with decoding skills, and she says she loves to read, but she has a very difficult time remembering what she read. "It just flies by, and I get to the end of the page, and I can't remember a thing." She has good ideas for creative writing and expresses her own thoughts clearly, but she does poorly on essay tests that require her to remember the details of a piece of literature the students have been assigned to read.

Difficulties

Students who have difficulties retaining material or recalling it typically

1. Do not process information adequately or sufficiently, often because of poor selective attention.

2. Lack effective strategies for grouping incoming information into smaller, useful, and interrelated units.

3. Have poor immediate or short-term memory.

4. Have difficulty recalling information quickly, accurately, or easily.

5. Can memorize and use material in one context or situation but cannot recall or use the same information in another context or situation.

Strategies

Several strategies will help improve the memory skills of all students. Memory activities are most effective when they are tied to the content to be recalled and least effective when memorization is seen as the goal of instruction. When the introduction of a lesson includes the repetition and review of previously learned skills and concepts, the students' understanding and memory of the new lesson improves. Students' discussions and activities help them retain and recall what they have learned. Students tend to remember better the material that they find meaningful than the material that they believe is irrelevant to them.

Strategies to facilitate students' retention and retrieval of material are provided in Table 2.4.

PRODUCTIVITY

This section covers students who process information more slowly than others and consequently complete less work within a comparable period of time. Like adults, some students move and respond more slowly than others, either by temperament or by disposition. It is also common for some people to become more deliberate and less active in situations in which they are unsuccessful. In addition, students who have difficulties in schoolwork and on whom greater attention is focused can become anxious and work more slowly than usual.

Table 2.4   Teaching Strategies for Retrieval of Information/Knowledge

Elem	Mid	Sec	Strategies
X	X	X	Include a preview and a review of the material to be learned during instruction.
X	X	X	Provide a brief summary of concepts or skills that were covered in the previous class, including the highlights of important concepts or features, to improve the students' retention of information.
X	X	X	Develop simple mnemonic devices to help students associate new vocabulary and concepts with familiar material.
X	X	X	Provide information in manageable units and help students group interrelated blocks of information.
	X	X	Teach students about the format and the organization of textbooks so that students know how to look for various types of information and resources.
X	X	X	Provide enough time for students to have both guided practice and independent practice for all applications of information.
X	X	X	Use visual imagery to help some students place information into a visual context. Diagramming, mapping, and drawing will also improve students' retention of information.
X	X	X	Encourage students to put information into their own words, check for accuracy, and accept originality and variety.
X	X	X	Demonstrate the connections between segments of information.
X	X	X	Assist students in organizing information through sequences, categories, and classifications.
	X	X	Provide frequent examples that have slight variations in the subject matter or focus.
X	X	X	Provide educational tasks that students find meaningful and relevant.
X	X	X	Post standards or objectives at the beginning of a unit of study and summarize the objectives at the end of the unit.
X	X	X	Provide incentives for memorizing realistic and manageable amounts of information or skills.

Difficulties

Students who work more slowly than their classmates typically

1. Produce written assignments that are shorter in length than those of other students.

2. Fail to complete in-class independent assignments even though they seem to focus adequate attention on the task.

3. Fail to complete drill exercises in the time allocated.

4. Complain of writer's cramp or discomfort in writing, which is caused by their awkward or tight pencil grip.

5. Take a disorganized, unplanned, rigid, or fragmented approach to problem solving.

6. Find that their ability to act is impeded if they need to make decisions.

7. Become fatigued from the effort needed to complete a presentation or assignment within a timed period.

Strategies

Reduced productivity often occurs because the student has difficulties processing, retrieving, or applying information. When students who have these difficulties are required to work faster, they often significantly compromise the accuracy or legibility of their work. Table 2.5 provides strategies to help students improve their productivity.

MATHEMATICAL COMPUTATIONS AND OPERATIONS

The mathematics of addition, subtraction, multiplication, and division are organized around basic facts, place values, laws or structures, and regrouping. Students who have learning difficulties in math may initially have difficulties in writing and reversing numbers. As the student moves from counting to basic facts and then to more complex computations (e.g., algorithms), he or she may experience difficulty at any level, and that difficulty often acts as a barrier to moving to the next level of complexity. For example, the language problems that the student may experience when

Table 2.5   Teaching Strategies to Increase Productivity

Elem	Mid	Sec	Strategies
X			Reduce the student's anxiety about performing a task quickly by making accommodations for more time or a shorter assignment.
X	X	X	Reduce visual and auditory stimulation around the student if distractions are the source of productivity problems.
	X	X	Allow students to provide essays or answers that are short but still demonstrate knowledge or skill.
X			Pair the slower student with a student who works at an average speed and who can assist in note taking or can model a faster pace that is acceptable to the slower student.
X	X	X	Provide a visual structure of ideas or events that the student can refer to when taking notes.
X	X		Provide opportunities for recording and listening to assignments if speed in reading or writing is the major problem.
X	X	X	Provide students with a computer and appropriate software programs to facilitate productivity, especially in writing.

using other skills, such as reading, may also interfere with learning the language and the concepts of mathematics. By paying careful attention to the level of math skill that the student achieves and the conditions that could interfere with that achievement, the educator can identify appropriate instructional strategies.

Difficulties

Students who perform poorly in mathematical computations and operations typically

1. Have difficulties in number reversals or writing numerals; they write slowly or illegibly.

2. Have difficulties in memorizing and remembering basic facts, details, and procedures.

3. Have difficulties when they are required to perform a sequence of computational steps.

4. Have difficulties when copying from the board or book to paper and lose their place when confronted with a page of computation problems.

5. Have difficulties in recalling facts, details, and procedures that they appeared to have understood yesterday.

6. Lack knowledge about mathematical language or terms.

Jason is a student in Mr. Marsh's math class. He knows his math facts, but it takes him forever to do a page of word problems. His work doesn't line up properly, so he frequently does poorly on homework or tests because he has brought down a number from the wrong column. Given enough time, he can be accurate in his work, but he reports that his hand gets cramped after a few minutes of writing.

Strategies

Strategies to facilitate students' skills in mathematical computations and operations are listed in Table 2.6.

MATHEMATICAL REASONING AND PROBLEM SOLVING

The National Council of Teachers of Mathematics has identified four overarching areas of mathematics: (a) mathematics as problem solving, (b) mathematics as communication, (c) mathematics as reasoning, and (d) mathematics as connections. For the purpose of this handbook, *mathematics as communication* refers to dialogue about mathematics between teachers, peers, and parents. The term pertains to generating problems, discussing problems and their solutions, and explaining procedures and applications. *Mathematics as connections* refers to the application of mathematics to real-world situations, to other subjects, and to other mathematical problems.

This section and the one that follows examine each area of mathematics but with an emphasis on the difficulties and the strategies related to *mathematics as problem solving* and *mathematics as reasoning*.

Table 2.6   Strategies to Increase Computational Skills

Elem	Mid	Sec	Strategies
X	X		Use computer programs to assist in drill and practice and calculators to give students an opportunity to correct and to check their own paper-and-pencil calculations. Select software programs in which students are highly interested, that provide positive feedback, and that offer a recordkeeping function when possible.
X	X	X	Use manipulatives (objects used to represent a quantity) whenever possible to help tie written numbers to real-world objects, volumes, and distances.
X	X		Facilitate games and activities that provide practice in the use of basic calculation skills.
X	X	X	Teach students to use calculators to assist them in multiple-computation problems and to increase the students' familiarity with the function of mathematical signs $(+, -, \times, \div)$.
X	X		Ask students to reduce the number of computational problems on a sheet of paper by covering all but one problem, several problems, or a row of problems to reduce distraction. Slowly increase the number of problems that are visible at one time.
X	X	X	Supply printed copies of the problems that are placed on the board to increase the proximity of the material to the student.
X	X	X	Use a copy machine to enlarge the size of numbers so that numbers printed in a small font size become easier to read.
X	X	X	Use graph paper that has a large grid or fold unlined paper to provide lines that help students define sections of the page and provide guidance for positioning numbers.
X	X	X	Review previously learned skills before each math session to refresh the students' memory.
X	X	X	Encourage the students' participation in all levels of the instructional process.
X	X	X	Provide demonstrations that use real-life examples to illustrate the mathematical concepts.
X	X	X	Suggest that students use colored highlight pens to highlight the symbols for different mathematical operations $(+, -, \times, \div)$ to increase the student's ability to recognize these symbols.

Elem	Mid	Sec	Strategies
X	X	X	Teach, review, and practice the application of mathematical language to increase the students' recognition and understanding of its use.
X	X	X	Extend the time on tests and quizzes for students who require extra time to complete assignments.
X	X	X	Provide problems that are targeted to the level at which the student frequently succeeds, encourage persistence, reward success, and show patience.

Difficulties

Students who have difficulties in mathematical reasoning and problem solving typically

1. Are unable to read word problems and need help to translate the problems into an oral, pictorial, or graphic problem.

2. Are unable to understand the complexity of language in word problems.

3. Have difficulty in identifying which arithmetic operations to use to solve word problems.

4. Are unable to translate a word problem into a computation format, even when they select the correct operation.

5. Have difficulty in moving from concrete, manipulative understanding to symbolic, written representation.

6. Have difficulty in estimating and regrouping even though they are able to do basic computation, select the appropriate operation, and complete problems on paper.

7. Have difficulty in creating a problem or discussing problems with peers.

8. Have difficulty in understanding proportions and relative size, especially in fractions and decimals.

9. Have difficulty in understanding fractions.

10. Have difficulty in interpreting arithmetic data contained in charts or graphs.

Strategies

Presenting problem solving as a group activity has merit as a strategy. Groups can consist of a pair of students, four or five students, or the whole class. Group activities provide ample opportunity for students to move through reasoning, communication, problem solving, and connecting. In cooperative learning groups, every member of the group can expect to be called on to present the group's solution to the class, making it necessary for all members to understand the group's reasoning and choice of procedure.

Strategies to improve students' reasoning and problem-solving skills are provided in Table 2.7.

READING WORD RECOGNITION

One of the most important skills that a student must master in school is recognizing words quickly and accurately. The beginning reader moves from the early phases of phonetically sounding out words, a skill that is also known as decoding, to a more skilled phase in which word recognition is effortless, fluent, and automatic. A student who has difficulty deciphering words of text accurately and rapidly will struggle to comprehend the meaning of the text, even when his or her underlying comprehension processes are intact. A student who experiences difficulty in word recognition must be taught to "crack the code" in an explicit, systematic, and direct manner.

Decoding entails using *word attack* skills, such as *phonics,* and *word analysis* skills, which enable the reader to separate words into parts, to determine the pronunciation of each word. Effective instruction in decoding depends on the teacher's knowledge of language construction, such as the relationship between sounds and the written symbol; knowledge of the ways in which children learn language; and knowledge of strategies for teaching alphabetic writing in a logical and systematic way.

To progress in reading, students must develop the skills that are prerequisite to fluent decoding of text, such as the awareness that spoken words are composed of separate sounds (also known as *phonemic awareness*) and the understanding that words are composed of individual letters and that letters have corresponding sounds (also known as *alphabetic principle*). Once students develop prerequisite skills, they need to learn common syllable patterns, word families, and morphemes (the prefixes, roots, and suffixes of the language).

Table 2.7   Strategies to Improve Mathematical Reasoning

Elem	Mid	Sec	Strategies
X	X	X	Provide students with a strategy for solving problems; for example, (a) "Read the problem and restate it in your own words," (b) "study and review the information that is given," (c) "choose an approach for solving the problem;" (d) or "try the approach and check the answer."
X	X		Post a written or pictorial sequence chart that shows steps for solving problems.
X	X		Alter the vocabulary and simplify phrases without reducing the number of arithmetic operations necessary for solving the problem.
X	X	X	Read a word problem and then ask students to sketch a picture or to demonstrate with a manipulative the situation presented.
X	X	X	Ask a student who has good reading and discussion skills to read a problem with a student who has poor reading skills. Allow the pair to discuss and solve the problem together.
X	X		Encourage students who display difficulties in understanding word problems to use manipulatives, create diagrams, or act out the problem alone or together with a group.
X	X	X	Use manipulatives whenever possible to recast a mathematical problem in tangible terms. Do not rush the transition from manipulatives to paper and pencil or to a calculator.
X	X		Help a student understand word problems by introducing small word problems. Slowly increase the complexity of the problems, check to determine whether the student's comprehension parallels the complexity of the problem, and return to an earlier level if the student's comprehension lags.
X	X	X	Develop problems that are relevant to students' backgrounds experiences, and interests.
X	X	X	Introduce one problem a week or one problem a day to be solved in pairs, small groups, or by the class. Check the students' levels of understanding during group problem solving. Allow time for slower students to understand the process and the solution.
X	X	X	Ask students to prepare word problems of their own by using specific operations and by moving to multioperational problems when students understand the simpler operations.

(Continued)

Table 2.7 (Continued)

Elem	Mid	Sec	Strategies
X	X	X	Provide an example of a completed problem at the top of assigned work sheets.
X	X		Assign students to reteach a unit, procedure, or process. Students' attitudes should be closely monitored to prevent any embarrassment or ridicule.
X	X	X	Provide extra time for testing, reduce homework assignments, and assign grades on the basis of the work that the student has completed and the progress that the student has made toward the class standard.
X	X	X	Allow and encourage the use of a calculator to speed up calculating time on word problems when the goal is to increase students' problem-solving and reasoning skills.

Difficulties

For many reasons, students may exhibit difficulties when attempting to acquire decoding skills. They may have a learning disability, such as dyslexia. They may be working in a second language, which creates confusion regarding specific phonemes. They may not have received proper instruction in the development of phonemic awareness, alphabetic principle, and other required fundamental skills (e.g., the ability to follow text and short-term memory skills). Whatever the cause, a student's inability to efficiently decode poses a substantial barrier to learning.

Students who have difficulties learning and applying decoding skills typically

1. Have difficulty in segmenting words into single linguistic units (they lack phonemic awareness).

2. Have difficulty in identifying or remembering the names of letters.

3. Have difficulty in learning how to blend sounds to form words.

4. Have difficulty in learning and remembering high-frequency-sight words that cannot be phonetically sounded out, such as *they, was, from, one, said,* and *have.*

5. Rely on context and guessing rather than rapid word recognition through decoding.

6. Are embarrassed or reluctant to read aloud in class.

7. Read aloud with a choppy, hesitant cadence.

8. Lose their place when reading, even when they use their index fingers or rulers to keep their place in material being studied.

9. Are unable to read written instructions or homework assignments without assistance.

10. Express a lack of interest in or even a dislike of reading.

11. Do not read for pleasure.

12. Introduce inaccuracies with letters and words when reading aloud. These inaccuracies typically are letter reversals (*b* and *d*); letter transpositions (*was* and *saw*); letter inversions (*m* and *w*); word omissions (dropping words, such as *and, a, the, for, to*); letter omissions (*steet* for *street, pace* for *place*); or additions, substitutions, or mispronunciations of words and letters.

Strategies

Students who have difficulties in decoding will require and benefit from direct instruction in the mechanics of reading. As students work to improve phonemic awareness and decoding skills, they need daily practice in reading material that is placed at a comfortable level for them.

Strategies to provide instruction in reading are listed in Table 2.8.

READING COMPREHENSION

Students who have difficulties in reading comprehension usually fall into one of several categories. Because some students struggle with decoding, their reading comprehension is adversely affected: The time and energy they spend decoding impairs their ability to retain information. For students who struggle with decoding, direct instruction in word attack skills often increases their level of reading comprehension by increasing their reading fluency. Actually, most students, whether or not they have reading difficulties, can profit from direct instruction in comprehension so that they can build a strong repertoire of strategies.

Some students may decode fairly accurately but seem unable to recall or to understand the message they have just read. These difficulties in reading comprehension are not related to difficulties in decoding skills but may be related to general problems with language. For example, students who are working in a second language may lack automatic decoding skills as well as the vocabulary development that is necessary for reading comprehension.

No matter what the cause, students who have deficits in reading comprehension will have difficulties remembering facts; sequencing pertinent details; and perceiving main ideas, themes, or other inferentially based written information.

Table 2.8   Strategies to Enhance Word Recognition

Elem	Mid	Sec	Strategies
X			Give explicit and sequential instruction in sound-letter correspondence (phonics).
X	X		Teach in a sequence that moves from speech to print rather than from print to speech.
X			Begin with high-utility, low-complexity consonants and vowels when teaching phonics and gradually move to more complex, less common graphemes, sound blending, and word families.
X	X		Combine phonics instruction with instruction in literature and informational text.
X			Accompany explicit instruction or systematic instruction with frequent, guided practice in decodable books. Decodable texts contain a high percentage of words with phonic elements and a high percentage of high-frequency-sight words that have already been taught.
X	X		Provide instruction in word pattern recognition rather than in rote memorization of rules.
X	X		Monitor a student's progress frequently and provide direct feedback to correct misperceptions.
X	X		Extend the use of decodable text as long as the student needs this practice to build automatic decoding strategies.
X	X	X	Ensure that the student is offered a selection of books at the student's reading level so that he or she can do individualized reading assignments.
X	X	X	Do not require a student with poor decoding skills to read aloud in front of classmates.
X			Consider reduced homework assignments while the student is gaining decoding skills.
X	X	X	Support the use of recorded books. Provide the student's parents with a complete list of books to be assigned. The parents will need to know the title of each book, the author, the publisher, the date published, and the edition.
X	X	X	Encourage the use of computers that run programs that are appropriate for students who have deficits in reading to enhance the students' understanding of the connection between reading and writing.
X	X	X	Make use of videos, which can be helpful when words are screened along with visual presentations.

Difficulties

Students who have difficulties in comprehending what they have read typically

1. Can identify the main ideas presented in the material they have read, but they do not recall pertinent details to support a position. For example, they may remember that the prince found Cinderella and that the couple lived happily ever after, but they may miss the importance of the glass slipper.

2. Can recall details but cannot summarize them cohesively or identify a theme correctly.

3. Work too slowly or too rapidly on reading assignments.

4. Show a difference in their ability to understand material that they read aloud compared with their ability to understand material that they read silently to themselves.

5. Fail to use contextual clues.

6. Read word for word rather than in meaningful phrases.

7. Display a poor vocabulary when responding orally or in writing.

8. Are unable to relate new information to material that they have learned previously.

Students who decode adequately or well but still display difficulties in reading comprehension may require direct instruction in various aspects of comprehension skills, such as vocabulary development, the use of semantics (cues for meaning), and syntax (structural cues in a phrase, clause, or sentence). Students gain clues to content by receiving instruction in the different elements found in narrative text (stories)—such as characters, setting, and plot—and in the structure found in expository text (nonfiction)—such as sequence, description, or argument and persuasion.

Strategies

A student who experiences difficulties in reading comprehension because of poor decoding skills will require direct instruction in the mechanics (the phonics) of written language. Strategies to facilitate reading comprehension for all students are provided in Table 2.9.

Table 2.9   Teaching Strategies to Promote Reading Comprehension

Elem	Mid	Sec	Strategies
X	X	X	Relate the major concepts in reading material to a student's experiences and interests.
X	X	X	Use diagrams or models to reduce the length or wordiness of written directions.
X	X		Record new words in a permanent place when introducing vocabulary. Next to each word, write a familiar synonym for easy reference.
X	X	X	Plan the format for discussions to accentuate concepts that students need to retain.
	X	X	Pair students for reading assignments when the lesson focuses on acquisition of information. Delegate oral reading to students who are strong in that skill.
X	X	X	Encourage students to highlight, underline, and box critical parts of the material being presented or to write in the margins of extra textbooks that they have purchased. You may even model highlighting techniques in a textbook from which a student can copy so that the student's attention is directed to the important parts.
X	X	X	Use asterisks, exclamation points, or other distinctive symbols to draw a student's attention to the most important points or steps being presented.
X	X	X	Be aware of the quality of photocopied materials. Is the print legible? Are the size of the type and the spacing of the text appropriate? Could the contrast cause eyestrain? (Consider photocopying work sheets on off-white or pale-colored paper to reduce eyestrain.) Is the student required to read one side of the photocopied material and to match up answers from the reverse side? (Often such back-and-forth matching further confuses a student who is already experiencing difficulties in reading comprehension.)
X	X		Block out information displayed on commercially prepared materials that is not relevant to the completion of the exercise.
X	X		Teach the structure of different types of written materials.
X	X	X	Show a video or film of literature being read and discuss it in class before and during the reading assignment.
X	X		Play in-class games with parts of speech. (For example, how many different verbs can the class offer that relate to human movement? Can the class construct a story by using these action words?)

Elem	Mid	Sec	Strategies
X	X		Familiarize students with symbols from a pronunciation guide. Then provide a sheet with new vocabulary words and difficult words that are phonetically coded to help increase the accuracy of students' reading. This method is especially helpful if a reading assignment is lengthy and expected to be completed independently.
X	X	X	Go over specific vocabulary before and during the reading assignment if the material to be read contains abstract, foreign, or arcane language (e.g., unfamiliar references and terms in Shakespeare's works).
X	X	X	Use computers with software programs that focus on skills in vocabulary and reading comprehension. Some software programs also offer speech enhancement to provide a multimodal or multisensory learning environment for the student.
X	X	X	Use graphic organizers to predict or to summarize information. For example, a matrix or web on pollution can be used to highlight categories (e.g., types, causes, solutions) and details.

SUMMARY

This chapter considers skills that students need to be able to learn effectively. These skills allow a student to receive instruction, remember what is experienced, process information, and acquire basic academic skills. Listening and attending are two skills that are especially necessary for learning, and teaching strategies can improve these skills. The abilities to organize and to remember also contribute to the learning process, are often weak in students who have low levels of achievement, and can be improved through instruction.

Both reading and mathematics are fundamental skills that are necessary for a student's achieving success in other school subjects. Difficulty in reading is the most common problem among students who have learning difficulties, and difficulties in math are also common. Early remediation can have long-term positive effects on a student's school performance. When a student's improvement is slow, the teacher must take aggressive steps to support the student's success by using the appropriate strategies.

INTERVENTION PLAN

Align your strategies with your instructional or behavioral objectives, standards, lesson plans, and activities. Select one or two strategies for each objective. Be sure to select strategies that fit your style of teaching.

For class or group instruction

Subject:

Standard(s):

Objectives:

Selected strategies:

1.

2.

For individual students who have learning difficulties

Subject:

Objectives:

Selected strategies:

1.

2.

Note: Educators may freely copy this page.

 # Strategies to Improve Performance Skills

This chapter describes the skills that students need to demonstrate what they have learned: verbal expression, handwriting and copying, spelling, written expression, and test taking. They are the foundation of academic performance and provide the communication tools that students need to express their knowledge through the spoken and written word. Appropriate social behavior also plays a critical role in a student's success in school and is both an interactional and a performance skill. The discussion of each skill consists of a list of common difficulties and a list of suggested strategies for improving the skill.

> Jaime is a student in Ms. Long's class. He is very reluctant to raise his hand in class to ask or answer questions. In fact, one day Ms. Long counted him absent because he was so quiet, she didn't even know he was there. English is Jaime's second language, and he sometimes mixes up his Spanish and English words both verbally and in writing.

This chapter considers the basic skills that are the foundation of success in such academic areas as reading, mathematics, social science, and science. The appropriate use of strategies can make it possible for a student who writes poorly to succeed in subject areas like social science and history; however, teachers must continuously work to improve their students' basic skills, which make independent student growth possible. Speaking and writing continue to be the primary methods for communicating knowledge and demonstrating academic skills in upper-grade classrooms.

Verbal expression continues to dominate classroom communication and is the major means of face-to-face communication in our society. Verbal communication is the public way that we express ourselves and the single most apparent way that a person's ability is judged in school, work, and society. The skill of verbal expression is a critical part of educational development.

Writing is one of the most important ways that students express what they know in reports and tests. Handwriting and spelling skills have assumed somewhat less importance than they once held in everyday life, now that the use of computer keyboards has reduced the need for clear handwriting and word processing spell-check programs supplement people's ability to spell accurately. However, legible and accurate hand-written materials are still an important means of communicating in the classroom, and "on-demand" writing is a critical skill that is required in some classrooms, in testing, and in job activities.

Social skills and test-taking skills are the last two topics covered in this chapter. Social behavior can support learning or act as a barrier to it. A certain degree of collaboration and cooperation among students is essential to all group instruction. At the same time, talking out of turn, clowning, leaving one's seat, arguing, and other disruptive actions not only interfere with other students' ability to learn but also distract the student from the learning tasks that he or she needs to accomplish.

Test taking is a skill that relies on the student's knowledge of the subject and on his or her ability to demonstrate that knowledge. There are test-taking skills that, once taught, can help a student's test performance, and there are alternative forms of evaluation that can accurately determine a student's knowledge and skill level. Both test-taking skills and alternative forms of evaluation are examined in this chapter.

VERBAL EXPRESSION

Students who have difficulties in verbal expression or expressive language are often unable either to understand directions and information that is spoken or to verbally communicate their knowledge, thoughts, and feelings. In large part, group instruction is communicated orally in the form of directions, discourse, and lectures. Being unable to fully understand the spoken word or to communicate with ease and accuracy is a severe disadvantage. Students who have developmental difficulties in verbal expression and those for whom English is a second language are at risk of failing in school.

Difficulties in receptive and expressive language may negatively affect the student's listening and social skills as discussed in this handbook.

Difficulties

Students who have difficulties in verbal expression typically

1. Are reticent to volunteer or participate in class discussions. They may be shy with peers or adults.

2. Have difficulty responding quickly to oral questions.

3. Provide answers that are short or clipped or that lack elaboration.

4. Use colloquial rather than technical terms.

5. Have difficulty giving clear and coherent responses.

6. Display poor mechanics of speech; for example, they have difficulties in fluency and sentence structure.

7. Have difficulty retrieving or using the appropriate word. This difficulty is expressed through word repetitions, reformulations, substitutions, or delays.

Strategies

Strategies that improve verbal expression are usually associated with the content, form, or use of language, and they consist of attention to vocabulary, abstract formulations, grammatical form and complexity, appropriateness to setting, and variety of use. The strategies presented here involve ways teachers can help students overcome or compensate for expressive difficulties. Table 3.1 presents effective strategies and the grade levels for which they are appropriate.

HANDWRITING AND COPYING

Students who have difficulties in handwriting and copying often have trouble writing legibly, or fast enough, or both legibly and fast enough to keep up with note taking, copying assignments, and answering essay questions. Doing homework that requires copying and writing is also difficult. These students are usually experiencing a neurological processing difficulty and are not intentionally being sloppy or careless. Rather, an underlying problem with integrating visual and motor skills constricts the students' ability to perform writing tasks or copying tasks efficiently or to do both tasks well.

Table 3.1   Teaching Strategies to Enhance Verbal Expression

Elem	Mid	Sec	Verbal Expression Strategies
X	X	X	Ask students questions when you know that they will answer correctly rather than posing questions to assess the students' attentiveness.
X	X	X	Ask students who are having difficulty answering a question that has multiple components to provide an initial response or to respond to only one component.
X	X	X	Ask students who have expressive difficulties questions that require short responses when the student is answering in front of the whole class.
	X	X	Provide questions ahead of time so that students can prepare oral responses.
X	X	X	Provide opportunities for vocabulary building and practice new words orally in a safe environment.
	X	X	Guide students into elaborating on their statements. Lead them into developing metaphors, similes, and idioms.
X	X	X	Allow students to use alternative modes of response, such as preparing written responses or demonstrations.
	X	X	Allow students to submit written scripts of their responses that can be weighted with their verbal performance.
X	X	X	Allow students to discuss a topic in pairs or in small groups before a class discussion.
X	X	X	Devise a clear and attainable structure for open-ended questions. For example, say, "Give me one way in which meteors and comets are alike."
X	X	X	Give students time to think (five seconds or more) about the questions that you pose orally. A student's delayed responses tend to be more thoughtful than his or her quick responses.
X	X		Give students a clue to the initial sound or letter of the correct answer and wait five seconds before you accept an answer.
X	X	X	Allow students to prepare a script. Facilitate the presentation by creating a forum, such as a puppet show (for younger students) or a television talk show (for older students).
X	X	X	Assign students to prepare tape recordings of their answers or conduct one-on-one interviews with the student rather than requiring public responses.

Difficulties

Students who have difficulties in handwriting and copying typically

1. Demonstrate chronically poor handwriting.

2. Hold their wrists, bodies, and papers in odd positions. They may hold pencils inappropriately, change their grip often, or write with too much or too little pressure. Their fingers may appear cramped on the writing tool.

3. Excessively erase or cross out material on paper and on the chalkboard.

4. Have difficulty in learning cursive forms and prefer printing over cursive writing. The quality of their printing and cursive writing may differ significantly. They may be unable to read the teacher's cursive handwriting.

5. Have difficulty in forming letters or letter connections automatically in cursive writing because they cannot recall the sequence of movements needed. They may display confusion between cursive letters, such as *f* and *b, m* and *n,* and *w* and *u.*

6. Write in a mixture of upper-case and lower-case letters, in a mixture of printed and cursive letters, or in irregular sizes and shapes.

7. Do not complete cursive letters, such as *i, j, t,* and *x.*

8. Copy slowly and inefficiently, with labored handwriting.

9. Draw excellently but find writing and copying arduous and difficult.

10. Display difficulties in fine-motor skills when they manipulate small objects or tools. Conversely, they may be talented in these areas; fine-motor skills do not necessarily transfer to handwriting skills.

11. Lose interest in or become easily fatigued by writing and copying tasks. Their handwriting deteriorates as the activity progresses. Homework assignments that require copying and writing are often very difficult for these students to complete within reasonable time frames.

12. Have difficulty in keeping up with copying, especially when the material is shown from a distance (e.g., when they are copying from a blackboard).

13. Have difficulty in spatial organization when writing or copying. The students' letters, words, and numbers may go uphill or downhill, or they may be cramped too close together or spread too far apart. The students' letters or numbers may appear distorted or rotated.

Students who experience many of the classroom behaviors in the foregoing list may be dysgraphic (that is, for such students handwriting and copying are not automatic functions). The student, teacher, and parent should understand this condition.

Strategies

The guidelines for teaching legible handwriting are to model, discuss critical attributes, give physical prompts, use verbalization, write from memory, and practice. Strategies to help students who experience difficulties in handwriting tasks are listed in Table 3.2.

Table 3.2 Teaching Strategies to Help Students Who Struggle With Handwriting Difficulties

Elem	Mid	Sec	Strategies to Help With Handwriting Problems
X			Provide instruction in forming and connecting cursive letters by using lined paper to show spacing and the beginning, medial, and ending positions of letters. Provide an analysis of how letters connect.
X			Evaluate dated samples of handwriting to track the students' progress and the need for assistance.
X	X	X	Have students whose work has messy erasures and excessive corrections, lacks neatness, and is poorly organized to use a pencil, to skip lines when writing drafts, and to make corrections in the spaces between lines.
X	X	X	Encourage the use of erasable writing instruments and erasers that do not tear the paper.
			Organize students into groups during writing activities so that a student can be paired or grouped with students who write legibly.
X	X	X	Encourage and support the students' development of keyboarding and word-processing computer skills.
X	X	X	Accept dictated material for homework assignments while a student is learning keyboarding skills. Have parents write *Dictated* on the paper and ask parents not to reword the student's work.
X	X	X	Make sure the student uses an appropriate grip; ask student to practice the appropriate grip 10 minutes per day.
X	X	X	Grade some creative-writing assignments for content rather than for mechanics to reward the students' thought and sustained effort.

Table 3.3   Teaching Strategies for Students Who Struggle With Copying

Elem	Mid	Sec	Strategies to Help Students Who Struggle With Copying
X	X	X	Minimize the quantity of copying work that is required to complete an assignment.
X	X	X	Pause periodically during a presentation to allow students to ask questions and to enable them to catch up with copying tasks.
X	X	X	Give students note sheets so that copying can be done at their desks rather than from the board.
X	X	X	Use a copy machine to enlarge labeling or fill-in-the-blanks spaces on prepublished handouts.
X	X	X	Allow a student who has legible handwriting to make a copy of assignments that is then reproduced for other students.
X	X	X	Use fill-in-the-blank sheets and mapping sheets to minimize the copying that is required when a student takes notes.
X	X	X	Avoid teaching through copying tasks and repetitive writing tasks, such as copying spelling words multiple times or copying long sentences. Use predictive word processors to minimize keystrokes.
X	X	X	Use accommodations; for example, reduce the homework load, extend the time allowed for taking tests or for completing group projects, and assign a student to record information.
X	X	X	Give some tests that include answers that are oral or demonstrated.

Strategies to help students who experience difficulties in copying tasks are listed in Table 3.3.

SPELLING

Students and adults who read poorly often are poor spellers; however, many good readers are poor spellers, leading one to believe that spelling is a more difficult task than reading. In an age of computer spell checks and hand-held computer spellers, problems with spelling are easier to accommodate than problems with reading. Nonetheless, poor spelling can frustrate, embarrass, and limit both youngsters and adults.

Difficulties

Students who have difficulties in spelling typically

1. Resist or avoid doing written work at school.

2. Produce written assignments that are short and contain sentences that have few words. The quality of the content is far below the students' level of knowledge.

3. Have a written vocabulary that is much smaller and simpler than their speaking vocabulary.

4. Make more spelling errors as writing assignments increase in length.

5. Achieve passing grades on spelling tests, but their spelling is poor or erratic when they produce original writing.

6. Misspell words even when they are copying text, or they have difficulty in using a dictionary.

7. Have difficulty in discriminating between individual sounds within words.

8. Have difficulty in perceiving words as units of letters or sounds that can be broken apart or put together.

9. Have problems with hearing sounds in their correct sequence within words.

10. Are unable to remember the visual appearance of words *(dorp* for *drop, dessert* for *desert, thay* for *they, wun* for *won, wont* for *want).*

11. Have problems with spelling according to the approximate sound of the word *(enuf* for *enough, kat* for *cat).*

12. Lack knowledge of the structure and logic of written language *(dropt* for *dropped, nacher* for *nature).*

13. Lack knowledge of the relationships between letters and sounds *(baf* for *book).*

14. Have difficulty in spelling short words *(thay for they, wen for when, bol for ball),* despite practice.

15. Have problems with transpositions *(gril* for *girl, no* for *on, own* for *won*); reversals *(ded* for *bed, dlack* for *black, qen* for *pen);* and inversions *(may* for *way, wnst* for *must, waut* for *want,* and *we* for *me).*

16. Have difficulty in learning homophones, such as *there, their,* and *they're,* despite practice.

17. Have difficulty in learning sound and symbol relationships for vowels *(langthy* for *lengthy, Septimber* for *September, difficalt* for *difficult,* and *spouled* for *spoiled).*

Strategies

Fulk and Stormont-Spurgin (1995) describe several strategies for teaching spelling to students, including teacher-directed and student-study methods. Strategies can also be divided into multisensory approaches, rule-based methods, test-teach-test procedures, word list procedures, and modeling and imitating methods.

Strategies to support students who experience spelling difficulties are listed in Table 3.4.

WRITTEN EXPRESSION

As the importance of written expression increases in upper elementary grades, students who have learning difficulties may fall even farther behind their classmates. Teachers help these students keep up by involving them in the processes of prewriting, drafting, and revising that prepare and guide students in written expression.

> Jason is a student in Ms. Wright's eighth grade language arts class. Jason is an active participant in class discussions and loves to clown around in skits, role-playing, or other dramatic activities. When it's time to write, though, Jason reports that "all my ideas just jump right out of my head." He also struggles with spelling and tends to use very simple, short words when he is forced to write so that he won't lose points for spelling errors.

Difficulties

Students who lack skills in written expression typically

1. Have difficulty in writing answers correctly on paper but give correct answers when they are asked to respond orally.

2. Have a written vocabulary that is more simplistic than their speaking vocabulary.

3. Have a poor knowledge of writing mechanics, such as punctuation, capitalization, paragraph organization, and overall coherence that

Table 3.4   Teaching Strategies to Help Students Who Struggle With Spelling

Elem	Mid	Sec	Strategies
X	X		Ensure that a spelling program includes direct instruction; is structured; and is an identified, not an incidental, part of instruction.
X	X		Provide phonics instruction in spelling programs.
X			Teach correspondences between sounds and symbols.
X	X		Use basic, high-frequency-sight word lists and include words that are within the vocabulary of the students and words selected by the students.
X	X		Reduce lists to lengths that students who have spelling difficulties can manage.
X	X		Provide direct instruction in the logic and structure of language, including single-letter sounds, vowel and consonant blends, high-probability rules, roots and affixes, and prefixes and suffixes, depending on the student's age, grade, and level of development.
X	X	X	Avoid teaching confusing principles side by side; for example, words that have the short sound of *i* versus the short sound of *e*. Avoid presenting word lists that contain confusing spellings (e.g., *receive* and *pierce*).
X	X	X	Provide the student with correction and feedback as soon as possible after the student makes a mistake.
X	X	X	Assist students in using dictionaries, computer spellers, and spell checks whenever the students doubt their spelling.
X	X	X	Grade the content of written materials separately from the spelling to reward thinking in addition to mechanics.
X	X		Have students learn to identify possible spelling errors in their own work and underline them. Teachers should provide the corrections.
X			Provide short spelling lists that capitalize on the students' learning.

obscures the clarity of their ideas and the reader's ability to understand them.

4. Write incomplete or run-on sentences that frequently include misspellings.

5. Demonstrate better test results on objective, fill-in-the-blank, matching, or short-answer tests than on essay tests or extended writing assignments.

6. Have a poor record of completing or handing in extended writing assignments.

7. Do not effectively use prewriting strategies, such as brainstorming, mapping, or gathering information.

8. Do not produce logical, sequential, or organized written products.

9. Have difficulty in following a writing strategy even when one is provided.

10. Demonstrate limited skill in producing sentences, paragraphs, or multiple paragraphs. Such students provide few creative, narrative, descriptive, or expository writing examples.

Strategies

Writing involves a sequence of steps and strategies. Many students who have limited writing skills failed to learn the steps when they were taught in class. Without knowledge of the process of written expression, students are severely limited in being able to demonstrate what they have learned and in being able to communicate in writing. Failure can usually be avoided when a student acquires skills in prewriting activities, drafting, composing, revising, editing, and publishing. Strategies to improve students' success in written expression are provided in Table 3.5.

TEST TAKING

Students who have learning difficulties often find taking tests to be distasteful, a public exposure of learning deficits, and a no-win situation. Not only do these students have poor subject-matter skills, but they often also have poor test-taking skills, an additional deficiency that can magnify the first one. These concerns are exacerbated when tests require significant amounts of reading and writing.

Difficulties

Students who have difficulties taking tests typically

1. Delay looking at the test paper, thereby squandering the time provided.

2. Ignore important elements of the instructions and misunderstand the task.

Table 3.5   Teaching Strategies for Students Who Struggle With Written Expression

Elem	Mid	Sec	Strategies
X	X	X	Model written expression by completing the same assignments that you give to the students. Demonstrate the steps involved in the writing process. Share your experience with the process and discuss the students' experiences.
	X	X	Provide and discuss an outline of a writing strategy or mnemonic for the form of writing (e.g., journalistic, creative, descriptive, or expository) that is expected in class during the unit or semester.
X	X	X	Lead students through the prewriting steps of selecting a topic, brainstorming, discussing, gathering information, and organizing thoughts by creating an outline.
X	X		Use teacher-initiated story starters or group round-robin writing activities.
X	X	X	Allow students to do creative writing assignments in pairs. Form teams so that a student who has difficulty in writing is paired with a student who has strong writing skills.
X	X	X	Encourage students to use drawings, diagrams, charts, or graphs to illustrate the assigned topic before they begin a writing assignment or to supplement written work.
X	X	X	Have students record their story, expository responses, or narrative by using a tape recorder so that essential thoughts and ideas may be preserved throughout the writing process.
X	X		Shorten the length of the writing assignments without lowering standards for the quality of the content.
X			Avoid focusing on mechanics when the written work is in draft form. Allow students who have difficulty in written expression to dictate to another student or to an aide.
X	X		Have students read drafts in pairs, in small groups, or with the full class. Direct students to make constructive rather than critical comments and suggestions.
X	X	X	Work with students individually by making specific positive and corrective comments on a student's written work. Describe the next step to more correct or effective writing for each student. Keep suggestions simple and focused on one concern.
X	X	X	Provide students with a proofreading checklist. Have them proofread their own work and then assist a partner. Students should concentrate on learning one new skill.

Elem	Mid	Sec	Strategies
X	X	X	Avoid comments that reflect value judgments about the effort or the quality of the work. Note positive features and a feature needing improvement.
X	X	X	Give students class time to work on written assignments so that you can observe the students' efforts firsthand.
X	X	X	Give students two grades for written assignments: one for knowledge of content or creativity and one for sentence mechanics.
X	X		Assist in note taking by providing students at the beginning of class with a fill-in-the-blanks outline of an upcoming lecture. Provide visual cues when you are emphasizing a point that needs to be recorded on an outline.
X	X	X	Assist in note taking by providing students at the beginning of class with written questions that you will answer during the presentation.
X	X		Allow students to audio tape or to present oral reports with a written outline or a written summation.
X	X	X	Ask students to write on every other line of lined paper during their first and second drafts of a writing assignments to leave room for edits directly under their sentences.
		X	Conduct the first edit of the students' writing assignments as a peer review by another student. Have the student rewrite the assignment by incorporating the edits and then present the assignment to you for the second review.

3. Lose their place when they move between the test booklet and the answer sheet.

4. Make errors in identifying the question or item to which they are responding.

5. Make corrections and erasures, even when these changes are not allowed.

6. Make excuses for not taking the test, plead illness, or fail to go to school on test day.

7. Spend an inordinate amount of time on one item or a few items and do not finish the remainder of the test.

8. Make wild or random guesses or mark answers in a pattern.

9. Ask questions out loud or attempt to get help during testing.

10. Give up before starting to answer the items and complete no part of the test.

Strategies

Tests are divided into teacher-made tests and standardized tests. A separate list of suggestions is provided for each of the two; however, strategies for one kind of test may be applicable to the other.

Teacher-Made Tests

Strategies to assist students in taking teacher-made tests are as listed in Table 3.6.

Standardized Tests

Strategies to assist students in taking standardized tests are listed in Table 3.7.

APPROPRIATE SOCIAL BEHAVIOR

Some students who have problems with social skills will misunderstand a social situation and act inappropriately. Their behavior is often interpreted as purposeful or malicious when, in fact, the behavior is the result of not knowing how to act appropriately. Negative and critical responses by adults and other students add to the student's confusion. The difficulty often lies in a student's misunderstanding of social cues, body language, or subtle verbal messages. The result can be the disruption of group instruction and the isolation of the "wayward" student.

Jon is a student in Mr. Taylor's Spanish I class. He enjoys learning Spanish, but he is terrified to be called on. He tells Mr. Taylor that the other students make fun of him, and he prefers to stay in the classroom at lunch rather than socialize with other students on the quad. He appears to have very few friends.

Table 3.6 Teaching Strategies to Enhance Student Performance on Teacher-Made Tests

Elem	Mid	Sec	Strategies
X	X	X	Conduct a review session before the test. Provide a study guide that highlights key terms and concepts to be included in the test.
X	X	X	Give quizzes frequently to reduce the quantity of material covered on a test and to enable students to recover from a poor grade.
X	X	X	Give credit for class participation, in-class work, and work samples when possible so that a student's grade does not depend entirely on test results.
X	X	X	Provide the student with opportunities to express knowledge of subject matter in alternative ways (e.g., drawings, skits, illustrations, charts, graphs, projects, videos, audio recordings, and demonstrations).
X	X	X	Administer untimed tests or allow students one-and-a-half to two times more time to complete tests.
X	X	X	State clearly the objectives of the lesson or assignment and the content of the lesson or assignment and measure the students' progress in ways that are consistent with the objectives.
X	X	X	Ensure that answers to multiple choice questions are not ambiguous. Provide choices that are clearly right or wrong.
X	X	X	Make accommodations when needed to reduce the student's anxiety and to obtain valid responses; for example, administer a test one on one, orally, in a special room, or at a special time.
X	X	X	Use testing formats that reduce the amount of writing required (e.g., short-answer, multiple-choice, matching, and fill-in-the-blanks).
X	X	X	Provide separate evaluations for the content, spelling, and mechanics of language.
	X	X	Administer open-note, open-book, or take-home examinations.

Difficulties

Students who have problems with social skills typically

1. Misinterpret or are unaware of nonverbal language cues, such as gestures, facial expressions, or tone of voice.

2. Violate unintentionally the space of others by standing too close when conversing but then react with hostility when their own space is entered.

Table 3.7 Strategies to Improve Performance on Standardized Tests

Elem	Mid	Sec	Strategies
X	X	X	Arrange for students to take tests in smaller groups to reduce the students' anxiety.
X	X	X	Give a practice test the day before a test is to be administered that simulates the kinds of questions that will be asked and the responses that will be required on the formal test.
X	X	X	Ensure that the student has answered the sample questions accurately and in the right places.
X	X	X	Allow students to underline perceived key points as they read the test booklet.
X	X	X	Allow students to use blocking instruments, such as blank index cards, to reduce stimulus on the visual field and to aid the students in keeping their places when reading.
X	X	X	Highlight even-numbered questions and answers (or every fifth question and answer) in the test booklet and on the answer sheet so that the student can monitor his or her matching of an item with its response number or oval.

3. Perseverate on a topic and are unaware that the listener is bored or frustrated.

4. Engage in attention-seeking behaviors that are out of step with the unspoken patterns or limits of the peer group.

5. Have difficulty in establishing and maintaining ties with their peer group.

6. Fail to express interest in the thoughts, feelings, and activities of peers with the result that they initiate irrelevant conversations and are mocked or ridiculed.

7. Find fault quickly, blame others, turn on friends, and require the rigid adherence to rules by others.

8. Have trouble participating in groups of more than one other person.

Strategies

The challenge to improving social behavior is to increase the student's social awareness and skill without being threatening or demeaning. At the time a student behaves inappropriately, the behavior can be stopped and appropriate behavior can be demonstrated, but this is seldom the time when new behavior can be taught. New behavior must be practiced to be learned, and the student can most successfully learn new behavior when he or she can practice it in a safe environment. For these reasons, strategies to improve social skills are often successfully implemented at a quiet time and away from a crowd. Programs on effective group social skills can assist all students in learning more appropriate and collaborative behavior.

Strategies to assist students in improving their social skills are listed in Table 3.8.

Classroom Management Strategies

Changing individual behavior in a disorderly or unruly classroom can be difficult. For this reason it is helpful to determine first what improvements might be made in managing the group. The classroom environment that supports positive behavior encourages (a) a sense of community, (b) a feeling of belonging to the group, (c) the knowledge that the teacher cares about the students, (d) a sense that students have the power to succeed; (e) the opportunity for individual students' skills to emerge and to be recognized; and (f) a feeling of enjoyment and fun around acquiring new knowledge and new skills.

Table 3.9 provides strategies to create a healthy classroom environment in which order, respect, and self-regulation are conducive to positive classroom behaviors.

Strategies to Support Positive Behavior

This section examines a positive approach to dealing with an individual student's behavior. The hypothesis supporting this approach is that a child uses unacceptable behavior to support acceptable ideas, feelings, and emotions. The process for developing positive behavioral support is designed to (a) define the student's behavior, (b) develop hypotheses for the communicative intent of the behavior, (c) identify the corresponding skill deficit, and (d) develop appropriate teaching strategies.

Note: Larry W. Douglass prepared the material in this section for *I Can Learn,* the first edition of *Addressing Learning Disabilities and Difficulties*, when he served as an education specialist on the Positive Behavior Changes project for the California Department of Education. We thank Mr. Douglass for giving us permission to use this material in this edition.

Support for Students

Over the years many research studies have been conducted to understand students' behaviors better so that schools can respond positively. As dependency

Table 3.8   Teaching Strategies to Promote Appropriate Social Behavior

Elem	Mid	Sec	Strategies
X	X	X	Discuss appropriate behaviors with the class if the behavior of an entire class needs improving. Develop rules, monitor the students' behavior by using positive reinforcement, and establish checkpoints, such as, "How are we doing?"
X	X	X	Review a situation alone with a student after a cooling-off period following an incident. Listen to the student's perception of the incident. Without criticism from the teacher, the focus should be, "What can we do so that it doesn't happen again?" or "What can I help you do to make it work better?"
X	X	X	Agree on an appropriate response once a student acknowledges an inappropriate behavior. Have the student practice both modeling and playing the observer part (behavioral rehearsal).
X	X	X	Practice appropriate behaviors in a pair, with the teacher and student alternating roles, or in a small group where students alternate parts. The activity can be extended to a sequence of behaviors also.
X	X	X	Expect reversals. Behavior change usually takes time, and new practices and new commitments are opportunities for more improvement.
X	X	X	Suggest the next appropriate action when a student lapses into inappropriate behavior: effective coaching can sometimes take place in the real setting. An example is saying "John, take your pencil and begin to work" when a student has impulsively spoken out.
X	X	X	Pair a socially ineffective student with an effective and respected student when the class is engaged in paired activities.
X	X	X	Ask a student who behaves inappropriately to stop subject work during that period and quietly observe and make detailed notes on what other students do. Make this request outside the class. Review notes daily with the student and continue for several days.
X	X	X	Allow the student to suggest disciplinary repercussions for repeated misbehavior once he or she acknowledges participation and some responsibility.
X	X	X	Work with the class or group to reduce peer teasing or ostracism.

Table 3.9   Classroom Management Strategies

Elem	Mid	Sec	Strategies
X	X	X	Establish a few basic classroom rules that are short and clear. Post them and review and discuss them regularly.
X	X	X	Establish clear procedures for making transitions between activities, subjects, or periods. Rehearse the procedures to help establish them.
X	X	X	Be firm and consistent in the application of rules, establish reasonable consequences, and avoid consequences that punish the student or the teacher.
X	X	X	Act attentively and respectfully toward all students. Thank and acknowledge students honestly and frequently as a group and as individuals for their contributions, effort, and progress.
X	X	X	Avoid sarcasm, ridicule, caustic comments, and comparisons between students or groups.
X	X	X	Direct your words and attention to what a student should do rather than to the student's misbehavior (e.g., say, "John, begin to write your assignment" rather than, "John, stop looking out the window").
X	X	X	Reward appropriate classroom behavior by giving attention to it rather than by attending to misbehavior (e.g., say, "I like the way this group is working").
X	X	X	Move toward a source of noise while continuing to work with the group; proximity usually is the best silencer.
X	X	X	Establish hand signals and other silent cues to remind students to return to appropriate behavior.
X	X	X	Excuse yourself from working with a particular student when noise is persistent. Fix your eyes on the disturbers and move very slowly toward them. Move between the students and ask the first noisy student to work on the assignment. Repeat this approach with the other students. Move away slowly.
X	X	X	Pose a question to the whole class before calling on an individual student. Ask new questions based on the students' answers.
X	X	X	Hesitate for a count of five or more when asking a question that requires thought; then accept the students' answers.
X	X	X	Provide work that is appropriate to the skill level of each student and ensure frequent opportunities for students to succeed and to be personally recognized (e.g., plan time each day during which students can review their progress individually with their teacher).

(Continued)

Table 3.9 (Continued)

Elem	Mid	Sec	Strategies
X	X	X	Establish a method other than having students raise their hands by which students can attract the teacher's attention and get assistance; for example, have students use a folded and colored card that stands on their desks.
X	X	X	Make easy work available at each student's desk to occupy the time that the student waits.
X	X	X	Provide alternative activities, such as dramatizations or artistic projects, that support instruction and allow task-related movement and fun while the students learn.
X	X	X	Provide students with opportunities to assist each other in improving their academic skills and in modifying their behavior.
X	X	X	Enjoy and celebrate individual and group learning efforts, successes, completions, progress, milestones, and transitions.

on punishment declines, replacement behaviors and strategies must be offered to parents and teachers of students who have learning disabilities and behavioral challenges. This approach has brought about innovative interpretations for all behaviors regardless of a student's ability or disability. Although this process can potentially benefit all students, it appears to be especially appropriate for students who have learning disabilities.

The Positive Behavior Support Process

Many students have learned unacceptable ways to express acceptable ideas, feelings, and emotions, often using nonverbal *acting out* or *withdrawn* behaviors for this purpose. These students cannot be faulted for having these ideas or emotions or for having learned unacceptable forms of expression. Parents and teachers are the ones most likely to encounter those unacceptable forms that children have devised to tell about their experiences, problems, and dilemmas. Parents and teachers react by labeling these expressions "inappropriate" and "unacceptable." From what is understood about students who have learning disabilities, educators can recognize these students' difficulties in language acquisition and learning. The struggle that educators and parents face is to help these students learn acceptable ways of expressing their ideas, emotions, or feelings.

The Process

The steps in this positive behavioral support process are as follows:

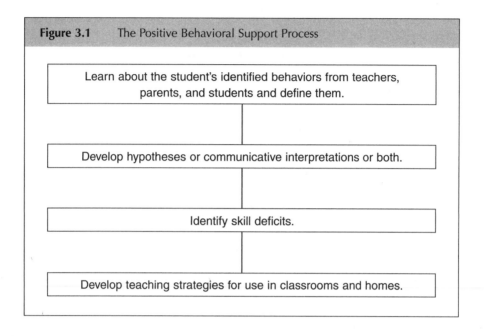

Figure 3.1 The Positive Behavioral Support Process

Learn about the student's identified behaviors from teachers, parents, and students and define them.

Develop hypotheses or communicative interpretations or both.

Identify skill deficits.

Develop teaching strategies for use in classrooms and homes.

Step 1: Learn about the student's behavior. This new process for understanding a student's behavior is based on four specific steps. To begin this process correctly, parents and teachers must honestly clarify the student's problem behavior. At this early stage, it is not important to critique the seriousness or inappropriateness of the behavior. It is, however, vitally important to pinpoint the behavior so that others working with the student can describe and recognize it. Being vague and general is not useful at this point. It is important to be specific. Exact descriptions will help teachers and parents as well as the student.

Step 2: Develop hypotheses around the communicative intent of the behavior. At this point it is useful to venture outside the procedures for normal behavioral analysis to try to find the possible communicative hypotheses for the identified behavior. Pooling their resources and knowledge, parents and teachers consider the intent of the problem behavior. It is best to use *I* statements, believing that the student is actually using his or her behavior to communicate. In this section, a common behavioral problem, talking out in class, is examined. The behavior and the accompanying hypotheses listed in the following example can be used to demonstrate the other steps in the process of positive behavioral support.

Behavior Problem	Possible Communicative Functions and Hypotheses
Talks out in class	I have an idea, and I must tell someone, so I . . .
	I don't get called on, so I . . .
	My ideas are very important to me, so I . . .
	I don't have a storage system; I don't want to lose my ideas, so I . . .
	I want to disrupt the class, so I . . .
	I am a good talker, and I want to be known for my strengths, so I . . .
	I know this really bothers my teacher, so I . . .
	I want others to lose, so I . . .
	I think and process by talking, so I . . .

The purpose of this step is to expand the thinking and the vision about the problem behavior. In most cases, parents and teachers have exhausted their strategies before they seek behavioral consultation. To counter this delay effectively, they need to increase the number of possibilities for understanding the behavior. At the end of this step, parents and teachers have added possibly dozens of potential interpretations to the list. However, this step must not be taken by only one person—either a parent or a teacher. The development of a full and wholesome list of interpretations depends on brainstorming by a group.

Before moving on, it is important to understand what makes this list critical to maintaining a positive approach. The good things about this list are that it

- is balanced (some aspects are good, and some are not),
- acknowledges behavior as communication,
- formalizes what most teachers do each minute or day,
- expands thinking about a student's behavior,
- links language problems and behavior in a student who has a learning disability,
- moves away from behavioral modification and becomes aligned more with teaching.

Before any decisions are made about a list of hypotheses, the list must be given to people who know the student well—teachers, parents, and the student. The chosen hypotheses become the focus of the intervention.

Step 3: Identify the corresponding skill deficit. The next step is to identify the skill deficit that corresponds to the chosen hypothesis. Examples of several hypotheses and the reasons for those choices are as follows:

Scenario A: A child's parents who select the hypothesis "I am a good talker, and I want to be known for my strengths" are granting that their child has a talent for speech. In addition, they are acknowledging their child's difficulty in recognizing additional personal strengths and skills. The child's deficit would be a lack of ability to see himself or herself as skilled in any other areas. The child is capable of recognizing a single strength—talking—but has a narrow vision of his or her other capacities.

Scenario B: On the other hand, if the teacher identifies "the student's lack of a storage system" as the hypothesis, the deficit would be defined as a lack of an organized pattern for mentally saving and retrieving one's thoughts and ideas. The child clearly has the skills for forming thoughts and ideas. But problems arise after those thoughts and ideas have been formulated because the child cannot hold those thoughts until later.

Scenario C: If the student identifies the communicative intent as "I don't get called on, so I talk out in class," the problem would be completely different. The deficit might be identified as the child's not recognizing times when he or she is called on or not recognizing how he or she could gain the teacher's attention and acceptance through means other than talking out in class.

As the preceding three scenarios show, hypotheses for different communicative intents may identify unique corresponding deficits. Nonetheless, the positive behavioral support process is strengthened by carefully selecting the appropriate hypothesis before parents and teachers move forward in their design of an intervention.

Step 4: Develop teaching strategies for interventions from the school and home. It is now appropriate to develop teaching strategies or curriculum modifications to affect the chosen hypothesis and the corresponding skill deficit. A return to the sample scenarios illustrates this step:

Scenario A: The parents' choice of "I am a good talker, and I want to be known for my strengths" would lead to the development of an intervention specific to this hypothesis. It would seem natural to assist this student in identifying and developing additional strengths and capacities. Being able to shine in other ways would allow the student to be more relaxed in his or her need to talk out in class.

Scenario B: The teacher identifies the lack of an effective storage system. The goal of the teacher would be to teach the student how to store and retrieve important thoughts and ideas. This activity might be accomplished with a pad of paper. Or the student might need a tape recorder to capture his or her thoughts and ideas. Whatever the intervention, it must specifically match the hypothesis of choice.

Scenario C: The student identifies the hypothesis "I don't get called on, so I talk out in class." Instead of waiting and hoping for recognition from the teacher, the student merely talks out whenever the need arises. A recording system might be designed whereby the student is responsible for collecting data on *times called on* and *times others are called on.* Likewise, the student might be shown how he or she could get the teacher's recognition by completing assignments and helping others. The goal of the teachers would be to equate these episodes with being called on in class. Once again, the student should learn to be more relaxed about the need to talk out in class.

This process has broad applicability for all teachers, especially for teachers of students who have exceptional needs who may have behavioral goals and objectives but do not require a behavioral intervention plan.

SUMMARY

There is no doubt that it takes more time to instruct students who have difficulties in written expression than it takes to teach average students. At the same time, strategies that teachers use to improve the work of poorly performing students often benefit all students. Students' failure to learn to express themselves through speech and in writing often reveals weaknesses and omissions in the instructional program that are not readily apparent in successful students. Weaknesses in paragraph construction, story line, and expository writing in average students often do not become apparent until late in the students' high school years or in college. Effective teaching strategies that address problem learners can augment and strengthen standard instruction and improve the skills of all students.

Some students perform slowly and are unable to complete their work; other students lack the social skills that they need to succeed in group settings. The lack of both productivity and appropriate social skills is common in poorly performing students. Strategies can be employed to assist these students in learning more effectively, demonstrating knowledge more adequately, and gaining from group participation. Teachers and parents have opportunities to observe a student in different settings and to determine which of the student's behaviors exist across settings and which are site specific. Working together and with the student, teachers and parents can identify effective strategies to assist the student both in the classroom and at home.

Testing usually occurs at a school site. Educators can modify classroom tests and can prepare students to succeed on standardized tests. When parents know the form of testing used in the classroom, they can sometimes help their child study in a way that produces better test-taking skills. Both teachers and parents need to recognize that testing is often an unpleasant experience for students who have learning difficulties; that the pressure of taking tests can reduce the student's accuracy; and that positive, realistic support is important in maintaining the student's confidence and effort.

INTERVENTION PLAN

Align your strategies with your instructional or behavioral objectives, standards, lesson plans, or activities. Select one or two strategies for each objective. Be sure to select strategies that fit your style of teaching.

For class or group instruction

Subject:

Standard(s):

Objectives:

Selected strategies:

1.

2.

For individual students who have learning difficulties

Subject:

Standard(s):

Objectives:

Selected strategies:

1.

2.

Note: Educators may freely copy this page.

PART II

The Special Education Referral Process

Referral and Eligibility

This chapter describes the process of determining a student's eligibility for special education. It contains information about reviewing general education interventions, making the referral, conducting the evaluation process, ensuring students' and parents' rights, determining eligibility, and reevaluating a student's needs for special education.

Good educational practice and federal and state regulations guide the process of deciding whether a student qualifies for special education. This chapter is not intended to include all the laws and regulations that govern the process; however, legislative citations are provided so that readers who wish to can locate source documents and read regulations in their entirety. Some of the wording used in the laws and regulations has been modified to fit the narrative style of this document.

The sequence within the IEP process contains the following eight steps:

1. Make general education modifications

2. Determine to what extent the modifications have been effective

3. Refer the student to special education for evaluation

4. Conduct an evaluation

5. Determine the student's eligibility

6. Create an educational plan

7. Review the plan at least annually

8. Reevaluate the plan within three years

Special education becomes an option only after consistently applied general education adaptations have failed to improve a student's behavior or his or her ability to learn. State and federal regulations use different words to identify a young person who has a disability. State regulations usually refer to the *pupil,* and federal regulations usually refer to the *child.* When *Addressing Learning Disabilities and Difficulties* quotes a regulation, it uses the term used by the source; however, the term *student* is used in the general text of this handbook and refers to children and youths who have disabilities.

State and federal regulations use the words *evaluation* and *assessment* somewhat differently. In *Addressing Learning Disabilities and Difficulties,* the word *evaluation* is generally used in place of the word *assessment,* except when *assessment* is used within a source document or is part of a commonly used term, such as in *informal assessment.*

DOCUMENTATION OF ADAPTATIONS

Educators are required to make general education adaptations before they formally refer a student for evaluation. This step is essential to ensuring that a student has had every opportunity to demonstrate an ability to learn or to manage his or her behavior before being formally referred. General education interventions must be serious attempts to alleviate a student's problems. Teachers need to employ individualized and group teaching strategies (see Chapters 2 and 3) that address the differentiated needs of students and are applicable to the general education classroom.

Before general education teachers seek assistance with students who have failed to achieve or who exhibit difficult behavior, they need to consider the steps that they have taken in the classroom to reduce the problems. Teachers should record their attempts to improve a students' performance not only to document their efforts but also to allow for a review of the effectiveness of each strategy. Such records can provide school-based teacher support teams with valuable information about the effects of various procedures. The following list can assist teachers in reviewing the procedures and interventions that they have already implemented and in considering additional steps that they might take to improve a student's performance:

Review of Academic Adaptations Attempted

1. Were tests or observations used to determine a student's skill levels, strengths, and weaknesses?

2. Were supplementary or alternative materials, texts, programs, and so forth used to improve his or her performance?

3. Were accommodations introduced to avoid the student's weaknesses and to support his or her ability to learn?

4. Were multisensory presentation strategies used to enhance the student's ability to learn?

5. Were collaborative groups, peer tutoring, and other peer support groups used to improve the student's performance?

6. Were efforts made by the teacher or by a trained aide to increase direct and individualized instruction to improve the student's performance?

7. Were collaborations with parents undertaken to remedy problems and were records kept of those collaborations?

8. Were data collected on outcomes of academic modifications and used to change teaching strategies?

9. Were notes made concerning the strategies that have been most successful and their implications for instructional changes?

10. Were the student's strengths and interests in and out of school identified for use in future planning?

Review of Classroom Behavior Interventions

1. What specific behaviors were most intrusive for the teacher or other students in or out of the classroom (e.g., speaking out, moving around, making bodily contact with others)?

2. What attempts were made to change the behavior (e.g., having discussions, solving problems, making contracts, practicing alternative behavior, "catching them being good")?

3. What were the conditions *immediately* preceding an incidence of each behavior (e.g., time of day, subject, participation in in-seat work or discussion, the use of text or work sheets, peer behavior)?

4. What attempts were made to change the preconditions (e.g., preparing the student for transitions, changing conditions, anticipating misbehavior, examining rules)?

5. What were the conditions *immediately* following a behavioral incident (e.g., class behavior, teacher behavior, student behavior)?

6. What attempts were made to change the results of the behavior (e.g., redirecting student activity, using planned ignoring, using corrective teaching)?

7. What were the possible purposes (intents) of the student's behavior and what efforts were made to provide for the student's needs in socially acceptable ways?

8. What were the attitudes of the teacher and the class toward the student and the attempts to reinforce or reestablish positive, constructive, and supportive interactions?

9. What were the effects of the specific interventions?

10. Which strategies were most successful?

Professional Assistance

Today's teachers face classrooms composed of students who are highly diverse in their cultural backgrounds, languages, life styles, economic situations, expectations, attitudes, motivations, and resources. Good educational practice requires a teacher who needs help with a student to seek assistance from other teaching specialists and from related educational professionals. These specialists and professionals include administrators, school psychologists, curriculum consultants, speech and language specialists, social workers, mental health workers, school nurses, and probation officers.

At times a problem that appears to be an isolated case may actually indicate a larger, schoolwide problem. For example, problematic classroom behaviors or low literacy skills may reflect school attitudes, procedures, and interventions. Professionals, such as curriculum consultants, mental health workers, or psychologists, who work outside the immediate school culture can help a teacher gain a broader perspective on the problems in the classroom and can alert administrators to schoolwide problems.

Education specialists and related education professionals can also provide teachers with useful assistance in solving students' problems. Because these professionals have experiences that bridge disciplines, they may be able to provide assistance in areas beyond their formal fields of expertise. For example, a curriculum consultant may be effective in suggesting management techniques; a school psychologist may be able to suggest teaching strategies; and a school nurse may have an understanding of family situations beyond health-related issues.

Student Success Teams

A student success team can be one powerful source of support for a teacher that resides within the teaching staff at the school site. Such teams may be formed on most campuses and can be an important part of general education. They provide a collective wisdom based on years of instructional and class management experience. The old adage that "two heads are better than one, and three heads are better than two" describes the core strength of student success teams. They can have a remarkable impact on improving teacher effectiveness and on reducing special education referrals.

Student success teams are known by a variety of titles, including *student study teams* and *student support teams* (Bullock & Menendez, 2001). The team often consists of a student's parents, the referring teacher, other classroom teachers, an administrator, other professional personnel, agency personnel, and, when appropriate, the student. On the request of a classroom teacher, the team reviews an individual student's problems, suggests alternative instructional or behavioral strategies that can be used in the general education classroom, recommends other teacher supports, and provides follow-up on a student's progress and the teacher's satisfaction. The core members of the team meet regularly, engage in structured problem solving, and focus on students' and teachers' needs.

The responsibilities of the team members are as follows:

1. The parents, when they are partners in the process, can share their child's history (e.g., developmental, health) and school concerns, provide accounts of effective and ineffective home interventions, clarify their child's past educational history, and participate in implementing strategies developed by the team.

2. The referring teacher and other staff members involved with the student share information about the student's strengths, the effects of attempted interventions, and their concerns about the student's progress.

3. The student shares information related to his or her difficulties and interests, identifies incentives that are effective motivators, and makes a commitment to try any solutions that are developed.

4. The team develops a collaborative action plan that contains strategies, accommodations, supports, and modifications that are designed to improve the student's success. Elements of the action plan can be used in the student's home, school, or community.

Personnel are assigned to implement the strategies, and timelines are designated for their completion. A follow-up date is set to determine whether the joint action plan effectively met the concerns about the student. This process can be repeated as often as necessary to ensure the student's continued success. Alone and then, if needed, with the aid of the parents and the advice of other professionals, the teacher attempts accommodations and modifications to correct or to alleviate the problem. The relative effectiveness of these interventions should be documented so that parents and teachers have this information for continuing reference. In addition, parents are encouraged to maintain their own records, which may contain information about attempted interventions and their effectiveness.

The success of a team often depends on the training of core team members and the support of the administrator and teaching staff. Reasoned judgments about a student's difficulties depend on specific information concerning the student's mastery of content standards in the adopted curriculum. Radius and Lesniak (1997) identify the following important areas of team knowledge and skills:

Knowledge
- Instructional strategies
- Behavioral interventions
- Scope and sequence of the curriculum
- Resources available in the school, the district, and the community for students and their families
- Group dynamics and social skills expected of students

Skills
- Listening
- Conflict resolution and negotiation
- Observation
- Collaborative decision making
- Leadership (p. 8)

Once a student's achievement history and the ongoing instructional interventions are analyzed, the team can make a well-reasoned judgment about referring the student for special education assessment. Subsequently, if the referred student is found to be ineligible for special education or for another categorical program, the school-based team can reconvene. The team's members can examine new information that was gathered during the evaluation process and develop new instructional and behavioral strategies.

REFERRAL PROCESS

A *referral* is a written request for an assessment to identify whether a student has exceptional needs. A parent, teacher, or other service provider can make a referral. A referral formally initiates a thorough evaluation in all areas related to the student's suspected learning disability. The evaluation may or may not result in the student's becoming eligible for special education or related services.

Sources of Referral for Special Education Evaluation

The student's teacher, parents, or school usually initiates consideration of the student's referral for formal evaluation. Typically, the referral is the outgrowth of a parent-teacher conference during which agreement is reached that the steps taken by the parent, teacher, and school-based team have not resulted in significant improvement in the student's progress and that the student's problem is serious. Agencies, professional persons, and members of the public can also make referrals.

Local educational agencies are also required to establish a child-finding system to determine whether there are students who have disabilities but who have not been identified. As the result of a child-finding effort or when school staff members believe that a referral is warranted, a parent conference is scheduled to discuss the child's problem and to obtain the parents' agreement on the need for referral. The parents must be provided with a written notice of the school's intent to refer, and the parents must voluntarily provide written consent before the referral process can proceed. Parents may refuse to give their consent. Parents may also revoke their consent, once given, but the revocation does not have a retroactive effect if the action that was consented to has already occurred.

Parents may also initiate a referral, and if needed, the school must assist the parents in completing the written portion of the referral process. In all cases, the parents' written consent is required for the initial referral for an evaluation, and the parents must be "fully informed of all information relevant to the activity for which consent is sought, in his or her native language, or other mode of communication" (34 *CFR* 300.500[b][1][i]). Parental consent for an evaluation is not a consent for placement.

Referral Steps

A written referral for evaluation is the first step in the special education process, and it sets in motion a sequence of time-determined steps. Within fifteen calendar days of the referral, the student's parents must be given a written proposed assessment plan. The plan must include an explanation of the parents' right to a due-process hearing and other procedural safeguards. Figure 4.1 outlines the course that is followed from the determination that the general education modifications have not been effective to the first meeting of the individualized education program (IEP) team.

Figure 4.1	Referral Steps			
The referral process begins when the modifications have been determined to be ineffective.	Parents, teachers, or students themselves may make the referral.	The assessment plan is delivered to the parent within fifteen days.	Parental approval of the assessment plan must be received. Parents have at least fifteen days to respond.	The evaluation is completed and then the IEP meeting is called.

EVALUATION PROCESS

Once the procedures for the formal referral have been completed, the evaluation process begins. According to federal regulations,

> Each public agency shall ensure that a full and individual evaluation is conducted for each child being considered for special education and related services . . .
> (1) To determine if the child is a "child with a disability" . . . and
> (2) To determine the educational needs of the child (34 *CFR* 300.320[a][1] and [2]).

The goals of the evaluation process are to (a) provide information that can be used to determine a student's eligibility for special education, (b) assess the level of the student's academic and behavioral functioning, and (c) develop an individualized education program that includes intervention strategies. The evaluation process should consider both the student's strengths and weaknesses, and it should provide a comprehensive understanding of the conditions that are relevant to the learning disability. Information gleaned during this process should provide clues to improving the student's performance. In other words, *the main purpose of the evaluation is not to label a student as having or not having a disability but to help a teacher educate a student experiencing difficulty in the classroom.*

The evaluation process involves the following elements and considerations:

1. The timeline

2. The assessment plan and procedures

3. Collection of needed data

4. Consideration of language issues

5. Qualified personnel

6. The IEP team

7. Procedures, materials, and tests

8. Consideration of other issues

9. The assessment report

The Timeline

As noted earlier in this chapter, before a referral for evaluation can be initiated, a student's parents must be notified and written parental consent obtained from them. A proposed assessment plan must be created and sent to the student's parents within fifteen calendar days of the referral. Once the parents have received the plan, they have at least an additional fifteen days to decide whether to consent to the proposed evaluation. If the parents give their consent, personnel from the local educational agency have sixty calendar days in which to conduct an evaluation and hold a meeting to develop an IEP.

The Assessment Plan and Procedures

A proposed assessment plan must contain information about the procedures, tests, records, and reports that the agency proposes to use as a basis for action. Good educational practice recommends giving the assessor or other knowledgeable professionals an opportunity to discuss with the parents the testing materials and strategies contained in the assessment plan. This discussion helps give parents the information they need to make informed decisions about the assessment plan, and it gives the assessor an opportunity to provide parents with details and to make changes to the plan.

The assessment plan shall follow these guidelines:

1. Be in language easily understood by the general public.

2. Be provided in the primary language of the parent or other mode of communication used by the parent, unless to do so is clearly not feasible.

3. Explain the types of assessments to be conducted.

4. State that no individualized education program will result from the assessment without the consent of the parent.

The written assessment plan shall also meet the following requirements:

1. It shall contain a description of any recent assessment that has been conducted, including available independent assessments and assessment information that the parents request.

2. It shall identify the pupil's primary language and the pupil's level of proficiency in the primary language.

3. A copy of the notice of parents' rights shall be attached to it (see the "Parents' Rights" section later in this chapter).

Collection of Needed Data

Collecting the information that is needed during an evaluation is a three-step process that begins with a review of the existing information. The review is followed by the identification of the data that need to be gathered to gain a full understanding of the student's problem, to determine appropriate interventions, and to meet eligibility requirements. Finally, all the people who are doing the evaluation are required to write a report (see the "Assessment Report" section later in this chapter).

The following paraphrase of federal regulations outlines the steps for determining which data should be collected during an evaluation:

(a) A group that includes the IEP team and other qualified practitioners should conduct a review of existing evaluation data during the initial evaluation and any reevaluation.

(1) Specifically, the data to be reviewed should include the following items:
   (i) Evaluations and information provided by the student's parents
   (ii) Current classroom-based assessments and observations
   (iii) Observations by teachers and related service providers

(2) Based on its review of existing data and information provided by the child's parents, the group conducting the evaluation must identify the additional data, if any, that are needed to determine
   (i) Whether the child has a particular category of disability
   (ii) The student's present levels of performance and educational needs
   (iii) Whether the child needs special education and related services
   (iv) Whether any additions or modifications to the special education and related services are needed to enable the child to meet the measurable goals set out in the child's IEP and to participate, as appropriate, in the general curriculum (34 *CFR* 300.533)

One goal of evaluation is to provide the referring teacher with additional information that might assist that teacher in designing and delivering improved general education instruction. If the student qualifies for special education services, the interventions and delivery of instruction are determined by the IEP team. If the student is found ineligible for special education services, the evaluation information should still assist the general education teacher, the student, and the parents in improving the student's performance. Knowledge gained during the evaluation process is applicable within the context of the general education setting. Properly understood, the information should translate into useful general education classroom strategies.

Consideration of Language Issues

The growth in the number of students whose primary language is other than English creates an increasing need for evaluation services that are appropriate for these students. To make informed decisions, the student and parents require access to readily understandable information. The law is clear. In situations that involve evaluation, communication, and decision making, the school is responsible for providing information and communications that are understandable to the student and to the student's parents. This responsibility includes making available school professionals who are fluent in the language of the student or of the student's parents or providing translators who are knowledgeable about and skillful in translating school-related information in the context of highly sensitive situations. Good educational practice also requires the participation in the evaluation process of assessors who are knowledgeable about cultural differences and their impact on the behaviors, attitudes, and beliefs of the student and his or her parents.

A main concern in all evaluation processes is the accuracy—or validity—and the consistency—or reliability—of the data and information. A family's difficulties with English can later invalidate information that was gathered by an English-only speaker who was working without a translator. Difficulties in comprehending English can persist even after an English learner appears to be fluent in English. Because a decision about special education is a serious event in the life of a student and the student's parents, every effort must be made to guarantee that decisions are based on correct information.

Several primary language issues should be considered within the special education process:

1. **The definition of a native language:** The term *native language* means the following:

> (1) The language normally used by that individual, or, in the case of a child, the language normally used by the parents of the child . . .

(2) In all direct contact with a child (including evaluation of the child), the language normally used by the child in the home or learning environment. (b) For an individual with deafness or blindness, or for an individual with no written language, the mode of communication is that normally used by the individual (such as sign language, braille, or oral communication) (34 *CFR* 300.19).

2. **Consent:** "The parent has been fully informed of all information relevant to the activity for which consent is sought, in his or her native language, or other mode of communication" (34 *CFR* 300.500[b][1][i]).

3. **Testing:** "Evaluations are provided and administered in the language and form most likely to yield accurate information on what the child knows and can do academically, developmentally, and functionally unless it is not feasible to provide or so administer" (IDEA 2004).

4. **Placement:** "The public agency shall make reasonable efforts to ensure that the parents understand, and are able to participate in, any group discussions relating to the educational placement of their child, including arranging for an interpreter for parents with deafness, or whose native language is other than English" (34 *CFR* 300.501[c][5]).

5. **IEP:** "The public agency shall take whatever action is necessary to ensure that the parent understands the proceedings at the IEP meeting, including arranging for an interpreter for parents with deafness or whose native language is other than English" (34 *CFR* 300.345[e]).

6. **Notices:** The public agency will provide notices in an understandable language. This includes providing notices "in the native language of the parent or other mode of communication used by the parent, unless it is clearly not feasible to do so" (34 *CFR* 300.503[c][1][ii]). For more information, see the "Parents' Rights" section later in this chapter.

The evaluation process may be conducted in English when the student is fluent in English. However, the classification *fluent English proficient* does not mean that the student functions better in English than in his or her primary language. Assessment in the primary language may still be necessary. English learners must be assessed in their primary languages. Baseline data regarding English language performance are also necessary. This information will help team members in developing appropriate educational plans.

Qualified Personnel

A question that parents often ask at the beginning of the evaluation process is, Who is allowed to administer tests to my child? Federal regulations state that standardized tests are to be "administered by trained and knowledgeable personnel" (34 *CFR* 300.532[c][1][ii]). Evaluators must be currently authorized to perform the services that are specified under their licenses or credentials.

The IEP Team

No one person determines a student's eligibility for special education or designs the student's individualized education program goals, objectives, and services. These duties are performed by the IEP team. A meeting of the IEP team must take place within sixty calendar days of the receipt of the parents' consent for evaluation, excluding the days between school sessions and terms.

The members of the IEP team consist of the following people:

- A representative other than the student's teacher who is designated by the administration, knowledgeable about program options, and qualified to provide or to supervise the provision of special education
- The student's current teacher, or another teacher who has recent knowledge of the student, or the referring teacher, or a special education teacher qualified to teach the student
- One or both of the student's parents or a representative chosen by the parent
- At least one person other than the student's regular teacher who has observed the student's educational performance, if the student is suspected of having a learning disability

When it is appropriate, the IEP team must also include the following persons:

- The student under consideration
- Other experts—at the discretion of the parent, district, special education local plan area, or county office—who can help develop the individualized education program
- A person who has conducted the assessment, who is knowledgeable about the assessment procedures, and who is familiar with the results of the assessment

Readers should note that once a student is in special education, and even though a special education class may be the student's primary placement, a general education teacher is required to attend or provide written documentation for all IEP meetings (34 *CFR* 300.344[a][2]).

The IEP team not only develops the written individualized education program but it also formally reviews the IEP at least annually for any student who is receiving special education services (unless the IEP team members agree that the IEP can extend beyond one year without IEP team review). In addition, the team must review the IEP whenever a team member, including the student's parents, request a review; when a student demonstrates a lack of anticipated progress; or when a student is being considered for expulsion from school.

Procedures, Materials, and Tests

Federal and state regulations discuss the need for a comprehensive evaluation of a student who is being considered for special education. Federal regulations state that in a comprehensive evaluation,

> (f) No single procedure is used as the sole criterion for determining whether a child is a child with a disability and for determining an appropriate educational program for the child.
> (g) The child is assessed in all areas related to the suspected disability, including, if appropriate, health, vision, hearing, social and emotional status, general intelligence, academic performance, communicative status, and motor abilities.
> (h) . . . The evaluation is sufficiently comprehensive to identify all of the child's special education and related services needs, whether or not commonly linked to the disability category in which the child has been classified.
> (i) The public agency uses technically sound instruments that may assess the relative contribution of cognitive and behavioral factors, in addition to physical or developmental factors.
> (j) The public agency uses assessment tools and strategies that provide relevant information that directly assists persons in determining the educational needs of the child (34 *CFR* 300.532[f–j]).

The scope of the evaluation must ensure that all testing and assessment materials are not racially, culturally, or sexually discriminatory. Because no single procedure can identify specific learning disabilities, members of the evaluation team must employ a variety of formal and informal procedures, evaluation materials, and assessment tests. Formal evaluation typically involves standardized tests, or *norm-referenced* tests, that are used primarily to compare the performance of the student with the performance of his or her peer group. Tests are usually selected on the basis of their technical adequacy, which is determined by the following characteristics: (a) validity, the degree to which the test actually measures what it says it measures; (b) reliability, the degree to which the test will give a similar score if the test is retaken; and (c) norms, research data based on the test publisher's sample of students. Tests are also examined for the possibility of ethnic, cultural, and gender bias.

Criterion-referenced tests are a type of informal evaluation that is used to measure a student's level of mastery of a particular skill. These tests determine the degree to which a student can perform certain academic tasks. In addition, a student's work samples are often collected and evaluated in combination with information gathered from criterion-referenced tests. Using both norm-referenced and criterion-referenced tests, evaluators identify the student's current level of performance, gain insight into the student's learning styles and strategies, and identify potential causes for the student's lack of academic success. Other terms used to refer to practices that are similar to criterion-referenced testing are *curriculum-based assessment, objective-referenced assessment, direct and frequent measurement, direct assessment,* and *formative evaluation of students' progress.*

Portfolio assessment, another effective tool, consists of analyzing actual samples of a student's academic work. *Authentic assessment* involves analyzing a student's progress by using tasks that are typical of the tasks that he or she would be required to do in class or in the real world. *Ecological assessment* involves evaluating the total environment that affects a student's achievement or behavior.

In contrast to formal evaluation, informal evaluation tends to be more behaviorally focused. Informal evaluation refers to the nonstandard methods that teachers and evaluators use to pinpoint a student's educational or behavioral strengths and weaknesses. The teacher uses nonstandard measures in the classroom almost daily. Results obtained from informal evaluation procedures can provide the qualitative detail often lacking in formal testing. The methods that teachers and evaluators use in making an informal evaluation include the following:

1. Written tests and quizzes

2. Behavior checklists, inventories, and rating scales

3. Class observations or outside observations

4. Orally administered exercises

5. Other demonstrations of students' skills

Test scores are reported in various ways. Standardized (norm-referenced) test scores are usually reported in one of five ways: (a) as grade-equivalent scores, (b) as age-equivalent scores; (c) as intelligence quotients; (d) as standard scores; or (e) as percentile ranks. Criterion-referenced scores and observations are usually reported (a) as a percent-correct score, (b) as a frequency count; (c) as descriptive phrases, or (d) as brief narratives or ecological descriptions. All forms of information can be valuable ingredients in understanding a student's difficulties and in constructing appropriate interventions.

Consideration of Other Issues

The influences of "environmental, cultural or economic disadvantage" (34 *CFR* 300.541[b][4]) on student performance and behavior are sometimes overlooked in the evaluation for special education services. Such underlying causes of poor student performance as "lack of instruction in reading or math" (34 *CFR* 300.534[b][1][i]) also can be underestimated. Societal circumstances and inadequate academic experiences are not justifiable reasons for special education placement, and an evaluation must weigh these issues. Failure to adequately assess in either area can lead to overreferral of students to special education and an overrepresentation of poor and minority students.

Documenting lack of instruction can be difficult; however, limited school experience and poor school attendance can be documented. Evidence of poor instruction is usually anecdotal. More valuable is an evaluation of a student's responsiveness to appropriate instruction and accommodations.

The Assessment Report

The persons who conduct an evaluation of a student must write a report of their findings. The written report is a critical element in the process of determining a student's eligibility for special education and is used to plan the individualized education program. The assessment report addresses the evaluation areas as outlined in the "Procedures, Materials, and Tests" section earlier in this chapter. It should discuss but should not be limited to the following topics:

- Whether the pupil may need special education and related services
- The basis for making the determination
- The relevant behavior noted during the observation of the pupil in an appropriate setting
- The relationship of that behavior to the pupil's academic and social functioning
- The educationally relevant health and development and medical findings, if any

- For pupils with learning disabilities, whether there is such a discrepancy between achievement and ability that it cannot be corrected without special education and related services
- A determination concerning the effects of environmental, cultural, or economic disadvantage, where appropriate

"Each team member shall certify in writing whether the report reflects his or her conclusion. If it does not, the team member must submit a separate statement presenting his or her conclusions" (34 *CFR* 300.543[b]).

PARENTS' RIGHTS

Although parental rights are discussed throughout this chapter, this section summarizes some of the procedural safeguards of parental rights as these safeguards are defined in federal regulation. States may provide additional rights and protections, and readers should obtain the regulations from their states.

Referral, Evaluation, and Change of Placement

The process of referring a student who is suspected of having a disability must provide assurance that general education modifications have been employed, and it must include the following procedural safeguards:

1. A notice to the parents that is written in a language easily understood by the public and that informs the parents in their native language or other mode of communication whenever the educational agency proposes or refuses to initiate an evaluation or to change an educational placement. When the native language or other mode of communication of the parent is not a written language (a) the notice must be translated orally or by other means for the parent in his or her native language or other mode of communication, (b) assurance must be made that the parent understands the content of the notice, and (c) evidence must be secured in writing that these requirements have been met (34 *CFR* 300.503 [c][2][i], [ii], and [iii]).

2. A written notice of an assessment plan that contains the following information:
   a. A description of the proposed action
   b. A brief reason for the proposed action
   c. A description of each proposed evaluation procedure, test, record, or report
   d. A statement on the voluntary nature of the consent to the proposed plan

   e. A statement that no individualized education program will begin
   without the consent of the parent

   f. A copy of the notice of parents' rights, which should be attached
   to the assessment plan

   g. A written explanation of all the procedural safeguards under the
   Individuals with Disabilities Education Act of 1997 and 2004,
   which must be included in the notice of parents' rights

   h. Procedures for requesting an informal meeting, a prehearing mediation conference, a mediation conference, or a due-process hearing; timelines for completing each process; a statement that due
   process is optional; and a description of the type of representative
   who may be invited to participate

Notice of Assessment Findings

Once the written assessment report has been completed, the IEP team
provides the parent with a notice of a meeting to review and discuss the
assessment results and to determine if the child has a disability and is eligible for special education services.

Independent Educational Evaluation

The following safeguards of parental rights pertain to the independent
educational evaluation:

1. The parent may request, at the school's expense, an independent educational evaluation if the parent disagrees with the evaluation obtained
   by the public agency (34 *CFR* 300.502[b][1]).

2. When parents request an independent educational evaluation, the
   local educational agency shall provide information about where the
   evaluation may be obtained and the applicable agency criteria for
   conducting the evaluation (34 *CFR* 300.502[a][2]). The agency can
   initiate a hearing to determine whether an independent evaluation is
   appropriate.

3. "If the parent obtains an independent educational evaluation at private
   expense, the results of the evaluation . . . Must be considered by the
   public agency, if it meets agency criteria" (34 *CFR* 300.502[c][1]).

Parents who request independent assessments may have those reports
considered as a part of the school's assessment process and the IEP team's
review if the assessment meets agency criteria. The evaluation process is
designed to accommodate the parents' disagreements, to allow for an "outside"

assessment, and to provide for the inclusion of additional assessment information.

Opportunity to Examine Records and to Participate in Meetings

State and federal laws give parents the right to examine their child's records and to participate in meetings.

1. Parents must be given an opportunity to inspect and to review all educational records and to participate in meetings with respect to
   a. The identification, evaluation, and placement of their child
   b. The provision of free, appropriate public education to their child

2. Parents must be assured of membership in any group that makes decisions on the educational placement of their child.
   a. The public agency must use procedures that are consistent with those required for IEP meetings, as stated in the *Code of Federal Regulations, Title 34,* Section 300.345(a–e).
   b. The public agency shall make reasonable efforts to assist parents in understanding and being able to participate in any group discussions related to the placement of their child.
   c. If neither parent can participate in a meeting during which a decision on the placement of their child is made, the agency will use other methods to ensure the parents' participation, such as conference telephone calls.
   d. If an agency is unable to secure the parents' participation, the agency must have a record of its attempt to ensure parents' involvement (34 *CFR* 300.501).

ELIGIBILITY AND SPECIFIC LEARNING DISABILITIES

Eligibility for special education services for students suspected of having a specific learning disability is based on criteria described in federal and state laws and regulations. When a student's eligibility for special education services is being determined, information from the referral and evaluation are used to assist an IEP team in making that determination and in selecting educational and behavioral interventions.

Federal regulations define what constitutes a specific learning disability (34 *CFR* 300.7[c][10][i]), and federal laws and regulations describe eligibility requirements (34 *CFR* 300.541). The determination that a child should receive special education is based on an IEP team decision that the eligibility criteria have been met. As discussed earlier, a specific learning disability is defined as

> a disorder in one or more of the basic psychological processes involved in understanding or in using language, spoken or written, that may manifest itself in an imperfect ability to listen, think, speak, read, write, spell, or to do mathematical calculations, including conditions such as perceptual disabilities, brain injury, minimal brain dysfunction, dyslexia, and developmental aphasia (34 *CRF* 300.7[c][10][i]).

To this end, the IEP team must determine that "The child does not achieve commensurate with his or her age and ability levels . . . if provided with learning experiences appropriate for the child's age and ability levels" (34 *CFR* 300.541[a][1]).

Traditionally, the IEP team has relied on an aptitude-achievement discrepancy in order to determine eligibility. IDEA 2004 provides that "a local education agency shall not be required to take into consideration whether a child has a discrepancy between achievement and intellectual ability in oral expression, listening comprehension, written expression, basic reading skill, mathematical calculation or mathematical reasoning." IDEA 2004 provides permission for districts to "use a process that determines if the child responds to scientific, research-based intervention" as part of the evaluation.

The response-to-instruction approach, which is beginning to be used more widely and is currently being extensively researched, has not yet resulted in a full-scale change in approach to eligibility. In a response-to-instruction approach, all students whose educational performance places them in an at-risk situation would be provided with early intervention services. Those students whose response to the intervention remained low would be deemed eligible for special education (Vaughn, Linan-Thompson, & Hickman, 2003).

For IEP teams who continue to use the discrepancy approach, the following factors are considered:

(a) A child has a severe discrepancy between achievement and intellectual ability in one or more of the following areas:
  (i) Oral expression
  (ii) Listening comprehension
  (iii) Written expression
  (iv) Basic reading skill
  (v) Reading comprehension
  (vi) Mathematics calculation
  (vii) Mathematics reasoning

(b) The team may not identify a child as having a specific learning disability if the severe discrepancy between ability and achievement is primarily the result of

  (1) A visual, hearing, or motor impairment;

  (2) Mental retardation;

  (3) Emotional disturbance; or

  (4) Environmental, cultural or economic disadvantage (34 CFR 300.541[a][2][i–vii] and [b][1–4]).

or

   (i) Lack of instruction in reading or math; or

   (ii) Limited English proficiency (34 *CFR* 300.534 [b][1][i–ii])

Even when standardized tests do not reveal a severe discrepancy between the student's ability and achievement, the IEP team may find that a severe discrepancy does exist as the result of a disorder in one or more of the student's basic psychological processes. A written report must accompany the team's finding of a severe discrepancy in the absence of standardized test scores.

Some unsuccessful students who have symptoms of learning disabilities may not meet the eligibility criteria for special education services under the discrepancy formula. These students may exhibit the potential to achieve, but they deliver a mediocre academic performance. Assessment procedures for these students could include curriculum-based information, such as portfolio assessment (work samples collected systematically from students), authentic assessment (tasks that are relevant to a student's real-world experience and assignments within the day-to-day school environment), and documented classroom observation by professionals.

Students who have specific learning disabilities but who don't qualify for special education services under IDEA 2004 may be eligible for necessary and appropriate accommodations within the context of a regular education program through Section 504 of the Rehabilitation Act of 1973. If a student does not qualify for special education or a related program, members of the IEP team should communicate these findings in a clear and usable fashion to the referring teacher, if the referring teacher was not present at the IEP meeting. A notation should also be made in the student's cumulative record for the reference of future teachers.

SUMMARY

This chapter describes the process that leads to a student's placement in special education. The process begins with a teacher's making significant general education accommodations and modifications before requesting a referral. The referral process consists of an assessment plan, the parent's agreement to the plan, an evaluation, decisions concerning the student's eligibility, and an individualized education program. Each step helps create a better understanding of a student's problem and helps identify the assistance needed to ameliorate the problem. Parental involvement and consent is required throughout the process.

The evaluation requires a comprehensive examination of the student's academic performance and behavioral conditions, the accommodations and modifications that the teacher made before the referral, and the student's current needs. Once approved by the student's parents, an evaluation plan details the tests, materials, procedures, and reports to be used to determine the student's special education eligibility and academic and behavioral needs. Written reports of all evaluation activities are required, and the reports are submitted to an IEP team. The IEP team reviews all information, determines the student's eligibility for special education, and develops an individualized education program.

The Individualized Education Program

This chapter discusses each of the components that make up a successful individualized education program (IEP); it describes the general process and content of an IEP and provides suggestions for conducting an IEP meeting. As noted in Chapter 4, the IEP team is responsible for determining a student's eligibility for special education and for developing the individual instructional and behavioral program. Once a student's eligibility is determined and the needs of the student are clarified, a continuum of program options, methods, and strategies are available to assist the student, his or her parents, and the school. The IEP may contain instructional and behavioral goals based on the student's needs. For students 16 and older, the IEP accompanies an individualized transition plan that contains instructional goals and plans for activities that promote the student's successful transition from school to postschool activities.

The Individuals with Disabilities Education Act (IDEA as amended, 1997 and 2004) contains important special education program elements that include the assurance that students with disabilities have the right to a free appropriate public education in the least restrictive environment. The act requires that each student receives an IEP and that there are procedural safeguards. The amended act also requires that fully qualified teachers serve children with disabilities.

Since the first Education of All Handicapped Students Act of 1975, the following elements have been established in all subsequent legislation, including IDEA 2004:

1. The right to a free appropriate public education (34 *CFR* 300.12 and *CFR* 300.300) is guaranteed to every child who has a disability in the United States.

2. Children who have disabilities are to be educated to the maximum extent appropriate with children who do not have disabilities. Removal of children who have disabilities from the regular educational environment should occur only when the nature or severity of the disability is such that education in regular classes with the use of supplementary aids and services cannot be achieved satisfactorily. [Adapted from 34 *CFR* 300.550(b)(1–2)]

3. The IEP outlines the specialized services and supports that students who have disabilities will need to be successful in a general education program. The quality and the effectiveness of the IEP depend considerably on the participation of the student and the student's parents.

4. The rights of parents and students to provide their informed consent, to participate in the IEP meetings, and to due process in the case of a disagreement are safeguarded in law.

5. Special education teachers who serve children with disabilities must be highly qualified teachers who hold special education certification or state licensure and meet the applicable requirements for elementary or secondary school teachers.

For complete, detailed, and current information on federal and state special education laws and regulations, the reader is referred to the appropriate state and federal regulations. The most current regulations often can be found online at state and federal education sites, national professional organization sites, nongovernmental Web sites, and through Web search sites. Resource B lists some specific sites that may be helpful.

INTENT OF THE IEP

Special education services are fundamentally embedded in the national guarantee of a free public education in the least restrictive environment for children with disabilities. The IEP is the basis for eligibility and program development, review, and revision. The IEP team manages the process, determines eligibility, establishes goals, monitors outcomes, and revises the IEP. Each step in the process is briefly described.

Establish Eligibility: The parent, a state educational agency, another state agency, or a local educational agency may initiate a request for an original evaluation to determine eligibility as a child with a disability. The parent must consent to an initial evaluation and a reevaluation and must subsequently provide informed consent before special education or related service is provided to the child. An IEP team, of which the parent is a part, determines if the initial evaluation information is adequate for a determination of eligibility and sufficient to develop an educational program. The team, with parental consent, can require additional evaluation information.

A reevaluation shall occur not more frequently than once a year, unless the parent and the local education agency agree; and at least once every three years, unless the parent and the local education agency agree that a reevaluation is unnecessary.

Determine Content: The IEP defines, in writing, a student's present level of academic performance and his or her annual educational and functional goals. The IEP also identifies how the child's progress toward those goals will be measured and when periodic progress reports will be provided. Also to be included are the following: special education and related services, supplementary aids and services, and an explanation for the extent of time the child will not participate with nondisabled children in regular class, in extracurricular activities, and in nonacademic activities.

Monitor Outcomes: The IEP team is required to review a child's IEP not less frequently than annually to determine if annual goals have been achieved and to revise the IEP appropriately. The IEP and the review must also be accessible to parents, the regular education teacher, the special education teacher, related service providers, and other service providers who are responsible for the program's implementation. Teachers and providers must be informed of their responsibilities for implementing the IEP and of the specific accommodations, modifications, and supports to be provided to the child.

Revisions: Revisions in the IEP are required when there is a lack of expected progress toward the annual goals, as the result of a reevaluation, on the basis of new information provided by or to the parent, in the interest of the child's anticipated needs, and other matters. The parent and the regular education teacher participate in IEP team meetings that consider revisions unless otherwise excused under other provisions.

IEP Team

Membership in the IEP team includes the following:

1. Parents of the child with a disability

2. Not less than one regular education teacher of the child

3. Not less than one special education teacher or, where appropriate, not less than one special education provider teaching the child

4. A representative of the local educational agency who is qualified to provide, or supervise the provision of, specially designed instruction to meet the unique needs of the child; knowledgeable about the general education curriculum; and knowledgeable about the availability of resources of the local educational agency

5. An individual who can interpret the instructional implications of evaluation results, who may already be a member of the team, as described in (1) through (6)

6. At the discretion of the parent or the agency, other individuals who have knowledge or special expertise regarding the child, including related service personnel as appropriate

7. Whenever appropriate, the child

SOURCE: Adapted from Amendments to IDEA, 2004, Sec. 614(d)(1)(B)(i)-(vii).

IEP MEETING

Meetings of the IEP team are intended to be nonadversarial and convened solely for the purpose of making educational decisions for the good of the child who has a disability. The child's parent or parents shall have an opportunity to examine all records pertaining to the child and to participate in meetings with respect to identification, evaluation, and educational placement. Prior notices from the local educational agency are required when the agency proposes to initiate or change or refuses to initiate a change in the identification, evaluation, or educational placement of the child.

IEP meetings shall be scheduled at times and places that are mutually agreed on. The parents shall be notified of the IEP meeting in writing and in their native language of the IEP early enough to ensure their opportunity to attend. The notice of the meeting shall contain information about the purpose, time, and location of the meeting; the names of who shall attend; and a copy of procedural safeguards. Parents should also be informed in the notice of their right to bring to the meeting other people who have knowledge or special expertise regarding the student.

If the parents have been notified of the meeting in writing and by telephone and if they decline to attend, the IEP meeting may still be held at the scheduled time, and the IEP may be developed. If the parents do not participate in the meeting, the IEP team members must document in detail all attempts made by telephone, in writing, or through visits to encourage the parent's participation. The completed IEP must be sent to the parents for their review, approval, and signatures. Program implementation requires written consent from one or both parents or the student's legal guardian. Check state and federal regulations for other actions.

CONTENT OF THE IEP DOCUMENT

The written IEP includes but is not limited to providing the following information:

DEFINITIONS: IN GENERAL—The term *individualized education program* or *IEP* means a written statement, for each child with a disability, that is developed, reviewed, and revised in accordance with this section in 2004 Amendments to IDEA, and that includes

(1) The present levels of academic achievement and functional performance, including
   (a) How the child's disability affects the child's involvement and progress in general education curriculum;
   (b) For preschool children, as appropriate, how the disability affects the child's participation in appropriate activities; and
   (c) For children with disabilities who take alternative assessments aligned to alternative achievement standards, a description of the benchmarks or short-term objectives;

(2) A statement of measurable annual goals, including academic and functional goals designed to
   (a) Meet the child's needs that result from the child's disability to enable the child to be involved in and make progress in the general education curriculum, and
   (b) Meet each of the child's other educational needs that result from the child's disability;

(3) A description of how the child's progress toward meeting the annual goals described in (2) will be measured and when periodic reports on the progress the child is making toward meeting the annual goals (such as through the use of quarterly or other periodic reports, concurrent with the issuance of report cards) will be provided.

(4) A statement of the special education and related services and supplementary aids and services, based on peer-reviewed research to the extent possible, to be provided to the child or on behalf of the child and a statement of the program modifications of supports for school personnel that will be provided for the child
   (a) To advance appropriately toward the annual goals
   (b) To be involved with and make progress in the general education curriculum in accordance with (a) and to participate in extracurricular and other nonacademic activities; and
   (c) To be educated and participate with other children with disabilities and nondisabled children describe in this subparagraph;

(5) An explanation of the extent, if any, to which the child will not participate with nondisabled children in regular class and in activities described in paragraph (4);

(6) A statement of any individual appropriate accommodations that are necessary to measure the academic achievement and functional performance of the child on state and districtwide assessments. [Adapted from 2004 Amendments to IDEA]
   (a) if the IEP Team determines that the child shall take an alternate assessment on a particular State or district wide assessment of student achievement, a statement of why—
      (i) the child cannot participate in the regular assessment; and
      (ii) the particular assessment is appropriate for the child;

(7) The projected date for the beginning of the services and modifications described in paragraph (4), and the anticipated frequency, location, and duration of those services and modifications; and

(8) Beginning not later than the first IEP to be in effect when the child is sixteen years old and updated annually thereafter,
   (a) Appropriate measurable postsecondary goals based on age appropriate transition assessments related to training, education, employment, and where appropriate, independent living skills;
   (b) Transition services needed to assist the child in reaching those goals, including courses of study, and
   (c) Beginning not later than one year before the child reaches the age of maturity under state law, a statement that the child has been informed of the child's rights under this title, if any, that will transfer to the child on reaching the age of maturity under section 615(m) [Amendment to IDEA, 2004]

SOURCE: Adapted from Amendments to IDEA, 2004, Sec. 614(d)(1)(A)(i)-(viii).

DEVELOPMENT OF IEP

IN GENERAL—In developing each child's IEP, the IEP team, subject to subparagraph (C) [Requirement With Respect to Regular Education Teacher in 2004 Amendments] shall consider

(1) The strengths of the child,

(2) The concerns of the parents for enhancing the education of their child,

(3) The results of the initial evaluation or the most recent evaluation of the child, and

(4) The academic, developmental, and functional needs of the child.

SOURCE: Adapted from Amendments to IDEA, 2004. Sec. 614(d)(3)(A)(i)-(iv).

CONSIDERATION OF SPECIAL FACTORS—the IEP Team shall

(1) In the case of a child whose behavior impedes the child's learning or that of others, consider the use of positive behavior interventions and supports, and other strategies to address the behavior,

(2) In the case of a child with limited English proficiency, consider the language needs and as such needs relate to the child's IEP,

(3) Consider the communication needs of the child, and in the case of a child who is deaf or hard of hearing . . . ,

(4) Consider whether the child needs assistive technology devices and services.

SOURCE: Adapted from Amendments to IDEA, 2004 Sec. 614(d)(3)(B)(i)-(iii).

Present Levels of Performance

Present levels of student performance describe the effect of the student's disability on his or her current academic or functional performance. Information about the student's performance is obtained from, but not limited to, formal assessments, classroom achievement tests, criterion reference measures, class and campus observation, and parent information and observations. Other types of assessment may be particularly useful for describing the performance of a student who is suspected of having a learning disability, an attentional disorder, or a behavioral problem. Nonstandardized measures, such as work samples, criterion reference tests, and information from parents, help establish the functional level of a student's performance.

Measurable Annual Goals

Special education services are meant to help a student succeed in the general education curriculum and meet state and school standards of performance. Educational goals are to be written to reflect these expectations. Goals describe what the student can reasonably be expected to accomplish within a year. They should be stated in general and specific terms that can be objectively measured. Goals should describe the anticipated accomplishments in the areas that need improvement. They should reflect the steps necessary to help the student gain access to the standards, skills, or competencies that are presented at his or her general education grade level.

A student should not be protected from exposure to higher-level concepts, standards, or competencies because he or she has not mastered a particular skill. Supplemental materials, aids, and accommodations can be used to help a student master age-appropriate or grade-appropriate skills. For example, a student should not work exclusively on multiplication facts in an effort to achieve grade-level performance standards in mathematics. The introduction of algebra sometimes assists a student leap forward in both math conceptualization and performance. The effective use of a calculator can allow a student to apply correct math operations to solve math problems without the student's mastering calculation. Similarly, a student who has poor reading skills can gain information and content competency about history from texts on tape or from the assistance of an oral reader.

Individualized annual goals and the short-term objectives or benchmarks that lead to the attainment of annual goals form the instructional steps between the student's initial level of performance and his or her attainment of appropriate grade-level standards. Individualized program goals and objectives should be accompanied by time lines to anticipate completion dates and evaluation criteria to verify a student's level of success in realizing the objectives. Periodic evaluation within the year is required.

Periodic Reports

Periodic reports can flow easily from a well-designed end-of-year IEP goal when the steps to achieve that goal are clear and measurable. Reports can be designed to include achievement, functional, and behavioral measures that are easy and routine to administer and record. Where possible, assessment should appear to measure what it claims to measure (face validity) and should be easy to describe to the parent and the child. Data recording and reporting tasks are often most reliable when they are easiest for teachers or providers to remember and manage. Memory and management can often be improved by selecting a specific time of day or day of the week for recording and selecting a quarterly or report card schedule for reporting.

Complications arise when instruction or services do not result in expected student improvement. The purpose of the periodic report is to monitor progress and provide an early warning to the teacher, provider, and team when the initial plan or the implementation needs to be modified. The teacher or provider should change strategies as they would with any struggling student and, failing at this, call upon support services to determine the direction for change. Significant change requires parent and team involvement.

Special Educational, Related Services, and Supplementary Aids and Services

The IEP specifies the specialized instruction, related services, and supplementary aids that will be provided to assist the child reach the annual goals. Team members determine the time, the frequency, and the location of the services that will be delivered to help a student. Also, the team determines the assistance needed for the child (a) to become involved with and make progress in the general education curriculum, (b) to participate in the extracurricular and nonacademic activities, and (c) to participate with other children with disabilities and with nondisabled children. In order determine the types of assistance needed for these tasks, the IEP team may need to seek expertise outside its normal membership.

Explanation for Nonparticipation

The IEP team must explain the extent to which, if any, the child with a disability will not participate with nondisabled children in regular class and in the extracurricular and nonacademic activities.

Services offered in the general education environment can provide the child with the least restrictive educational environment to the extent that the child can make progress in that environment. An IEP that successfully supports the child through specialized instruction, supplemental aids, and services in the general education classroom can help that child access and succeed in the general curriculum. A child with disabilities who, together with his or her peers, achieves within the general education curriculum has a reasonable chance to (a) meet grade-level standards, (b) participate in statewide assessments, (c) pass high school exit exams (d) and earn a general diploma, and (e) be prepared for postsecondary education or work. In addition, offering services to a child in the classroom environment provides an opportunity for maximum interaction between a student with a disability and his or her nondisabled peers in academic, extracurricular, and nonacademic activities. This is an expected goal for most children with learning disabilities.

The success of such a program depends on the quality of the plan and the implementation, the collaboration with the general education teacher, support of the parents, the careful monitoring of the child's progress, and a creative, timely response to a problem.

Ultimately, services must be determined by the student's need as determined in the IEP and not determined on the availability of a program or services. The reason that the student is removed from the general education classroom and the amount of time that the student will spend in the general education program must be stated in the IEP and explained in writing. Related services, transportation, and counseling must also be provided at public expense if the team determines that these services are needed to meet the educational goals of the IEP.

The IEP team should determine annually whether the student's level of performance would allow him or her to exit from the current program option into a less restrictive option. If the student can make the transition, exit criteria should be developed, and a plan for facilitating the transition between program options should be developed, the parent consulted, and a team decision made.

Accommodations and Assessments

Federal regulation (34 *CFR* 300.138–139, Amendments to IDEA 2004) requires students who have disabilities to be included in statewide (or districtwide) assessment programs that provide appropriate accommodations and modifications. The state is further required to provide an alternate assessment for students whose disabilities prevent them from participating in the general statewide assessment program. The Individuals with Disabilities Education Act requires all students to be included in either a statewide assessment or an alternate assessment. The IEP team determines which assessment should be used and which accommodations or modifications the student will need to participate in that assessment. It is not a question of *whether* students who have disabilities will participate in statewide assessments but *how* they will participate. States vary in their response to this requirement, and the guidelines for the state of residence will guide the IEP team and the local education agency.

The accommodations that students typically use during instruction may be used in a testing situation to allow the students to demonstrate their levels of achievement and skill without being impeded by the barriers that result from their disabilities. Accommodations can not change the content of the test, compensate for knowledge and abilities that the student has not acquired, or provide an unfair advantage over other students taking the test. For example, using braille or large print when a student is visually impaired may give the student equal access to the content of a test without interfering with the content itself. Allowing the student to record or dictate responses might be an appropriate accommodation when a student has a motor, perceptual, or writing problem that impedes the student's ability to write answers to questions or to perform tasks.

Testing accommodations may consist of variations in scheduling, setting, test format, and test directions and the use of aids, human helpers, or both. Testing accommodations may also include one or more of the following items:

- The ways in which the test items are explained to the students
- The methods that the students use to record their answers or responses
- Changes in the time schedule for administering subtests
- The location or setting in which the students take the test

As noted, alternate assessments may be provided for students who are unable to participate in the regular statewide assessment. An exemption from participation in the general statewide assessment is made for the relatively few students who have severe disabilities and for whom no adequate accommodation can be found. The IEP team must prepare a statement explaining why the student is to be exempted from the general statewide assessment and why the alternate assessment is to be provided.

Beginning of Services and Their Frequency, Location, and Duration

The IEP team decides the details of each child's educational program. These details include the following: (a) when the program is to begin; (b) how often interventions or strategies are to take place; (c) the location of the instruction or other service (e.g., whether instruction will occur within the general education classroom or a resource room); and (d) how long the intervention, strategy, or service will last. The team is accountable for carefully considering the details of the student's program and for making monitoring possible.

Evaluation Procedures

An evaluation procedure is the second step in planning for accountability. After the frequency, location, and duration of the intervention, strategy, or service are set, the IEP team determines the procedure for evaluating the student's progress. The law specifies that goals must be determined for each student's program and that schedules must be established for an annual year-end IEP review. In addition, periodic evaluation must take place at predetermined intervals within the year, and parents of a child with a disability are to be informed of their child's progress.

Statement That Student Has Been Informed of Rights

Beginning at least one year before a student with a disability reaches the age of majority (an age established by each state), a statement concerning the student's rights will be added to the IEP. This statement indicates that the student and his or her parents have been informed that all rights accorded to the parent shall transfer to the student when he or she reaches the age of majority. The student who reaches that age and whose parents have not obtained legal conservatorship will receive, along with his or her parents, any notices of safeguards. Furthermore, on reaching the age of majority, the student has the right to make educational decisions previously made by the parent.

Statement That Parents Shall Be Informed

At a minimum, parents must be notified in writing of a proposal for an initial evaluation and all subsequent IEP meetings. The initial notice and yearly written notifications will include a statement of the parents' rights. Notifications are to be in the language of the parents' primary language. IEP notifications must contain information about the purpose, the time, and the location of the meeting and the names of the participants. Parents have the right to attend, and are encouraged to, a meeting at a mutually agreed-on time and place.

Parents' regular inclusion in the implementation of the IEP is advisable. Parents can provide the student with support toward achieving the instructional goals and objectives of the plan. Parents can also provide the IEP team with valuable observations and recommendations during the review process. When the notice of the IEP meeting is sent to the parents, a form might be enclosed suggesting that the parents write down their observations about their child's progress along with their thoughts, questions, comments, and suggestions that they want to consider in the IEP meeting. By making these notes, parents can prepare for the IEP meeting as the experts on their child.

A list of the names, positions, and signatures of the IEP team members who attend the meeting and the date of the meeting must appear on the IEP form. If the parents agree to the plan, their signatures must also appear on the form. Parents are allowed to take the form home to consider the assessment information and the plan before they sign, but no one is legally able to sign the form unless he or she attends the actual meeting. No services may be delivered until the parents have given their written consent on the form. Agency recourse in response to a parent's refusal to consent is described in federal and state regulations. Variations in the items to be included on IEP forms and actual procedures may vary between states.

Transition Services

Several types of transitions are particularly relevant to making IEP decisions for students who have disabilities. One point of transition is the period of time in which a young child moves from Part C (Infant) of the Federal law into preschool and is in an age range that is outside the scope of this document. A second type of transition occurs when a student moves from special education into general education. The third occurs when a student prepares to move from school to postschool activities.

In preparation for the child's transition to a general education classroom or when the amount of special education services will be reduced, the IEP must contain a description of the activities that will assist in the integration of the child into the new class. The document should detail the nature of each activity, the time spent on the activity each day or week, and the activities that support a student's move from special education to general education. The intention of transition planning is to integrate, rather than place, the child into a general education setting.

The primary use of the term *transition* describes a period of time when the child prepares to move from school to postschool activities. Beginning not later than the first IEP to be in effect when the child turns sixteen and updated annually thereafter, the IEP must include postsecondary goals that are based on age-appropriate transition assessments related to training, educational employment, and where appropriate, independent living skills. The plan also needs to address the transition services (including courses of study) needed to assist the child to reach those goals.

THE POSITIVE BEHAVIORAL INTERVENTION PLAN

Moderate behavior problems often respond to teaching strategies that are designed to improve students' learning and performance. Student success teams or other school-based support teams can effectively assist teachers in applying appropriate instruction and management strategies. These teams have the advantage of providing group problem solving and on-site support. Improvements in the student's academic skills often lead to improvements in the student's motivation and behavior.

Some special education students do not respond to the teaching strategies developed by related service personnel and on-site teams of general and special educators, and these children continue to have serious behavioral problems. When these problems interfere with a child's ability to meet the goals and objectives that have been designated in his or her IEP, the IEP team must address these problems by conducting a behavioral analysis and developing a positive behavior intervention plan.

Federal and state laws and regulations outline the actions that educators may take when faced with difficult behavior from students who have disabilities. Federal regulation states that the individualized education program team shall "in the case of a child whose behavior impedes his or her learning or that of others, consider, if appropriate, strategies, including positive behavioral interventions, strategies, and supports to address that behavior" (34 *CFR* 300.346[a][2][i]). States and local educational agencies are required to describe the strategies that they will use to assist teachers and others in working to improve the students' behavior. Under unique circumstances school personnel may remove a child with a disability from school and place on suspension, in an alternative school, or another setting (this is described more fully in a subsequent section).

The IEP team is responsible for ensuring the implementation of the activities contained in a behavioral intervention plan. Interventions are designed to replace maladaptive behaviors with alternative acceptable behaviors. The focus is on providing positive behavioral support that improves a student's behavior and school performance.

The positive approach to behavioral intervention is intended to assist a child to develop new ways of acting that meet the student's needs and that increase his or her learning. The process begins with defining the behavioral problem, then moves to examining alternative behaviors, developing a behavioral intervention plan, implementing the interventions, and supporting and reviewing the implementation.

The general process for developing positive behavioral support contains the following steps:

1. Define the student's behavior with attention to the events that preceded the problem behavior and its function or communicative intent.

2. Assess the environment, teaching strategies, alternative behaviors, and reinforcers that help define behaviors and provide information for planning.

3. Assemble information and hold an IEP meeting during which the IEP team designs a positive behavioral intervention plan that outlines specific roles, responsibilities, behavior teaching strategies, and anticipated outcomes.

4. Provide assistance to help parents, teachers, and related personnel carry out positive behavioral plans. Establish periodic follow-up reviews and required reviews.

PLACEMENT IN ALTERNATIVE EDUCATION SETTINGS

School personnel may consider any unique circumstances on a case-by-case basis when determining whether to order a change in placement of a child with a disability who violates a code of child conduct. School personnel may remove the child from the current placement to an appropriate interim alternative educational setting, a licensed nonpublic school or agency setting, or suspension for not more than ten school days (to the extent that such alternatives are applied to children without disabilities). If school personnel seek a change in placement that would exceed ten days and the behavior that gave rise to the violation is determined not to be a manifestation of the disability, the relevant procedures applicable to children without disabilities may be applied.

A child with a disability (irrespective of whether the behavior is determined to be a manifestation of the child's disability) placed in another setting is to continue to receive educational services so as to participate in the general education curriculum and to progress toward meeting the goals set out in the IEP.

Manifestation determination is to be made in ten school days by a team including a representative of the local education agency, the parent, and relevant members of the IEP team. A review of information will include relevant information from the student's file, including the child's IEP, teacher observations, and any relevant information provided by the parent. Manifestation determination will be made if (a) the conduct in question was caused by, or had a direct and substantial relationship to, the child's disability; or (b) the conduct in question was the direct result of the local educational agency's failure to implement the IEP.

If the IEP team determines a manifestation, the team will provide a functional behavioral assessment if none exists and a modification if one is in existence. Unless there is an agreement between the local educational agency and the parent to a change of placement or there is a "special circumstance," the child is returned to the classroom with the new behavioral assessment.

Special circumstances include one of the following actions while at school, on school premises, or at a school function under the jurisdiction of the state or local agency: (a) is carrying or has possession of a weapon . . . ; (b) knowingly possesses or uses illegal drugs or sells or solicits the sale of a controlled substance . . . , (c) has inflicted seriously bodily injury upon another person . . . [brief adaptation from Amendments to IDEA, 2004, Sec. 615(k)(1)(B)(1)].

REVIEWS AND REEVALUATIONS

Reviews of an IEP occur yearly, and evaluations are based on periodic and annual reports. Additional information also can be requested by the team.

Reevaluations of children who have disabilities commonly occur under one of the following circumstances:

- When the conditions warrant a reevaluation
- When the child's parents or teacher request a reevaluation
- At least once every three years (triennially), as required by law (Adapted from 34 *CFR* 300.536[b])

During a reevaluation, the IEP team and other qualified professionals review existing assessment data, classroom assessments and observations, observations of teachers and related service providers, and comments from parents. If the team determines that further evaluation is necessary, the educational agency shall administer the necessary evaluation. The team then evaluates the following five elements:

1. The continued presence of a disability

2. The present levels of performance and the educational needs of the child

3. The additions or modifications needed to enable the child to meet the measurable goals of the IEP and to participate, as appropriate, in the general curriculum

4. The child's progress toward district standards and graduation requirements

5. Appropriate test accommodations or modifications that will allow the child to participate in districtwide and statewide assessments,

Procedural safeguards for reevaluations are the same as those required for initial evaluations.

SUMMARY

The question is sometimes asked, Why is special education "special"? It is special because it provides an IEP that is developed to meet the unique needs of a child. It recognizes that a child with disabilities may need specialized instruction, related service assistance, and supplementary aid and services to attain grade-level standards, to succeed on class, district, and state tests, to pass high school exit exams, to earn a high school diploma, and to succeed in postschool activities. The IEP identifies the needs of the individual child, develops a plan to deliver the necessary instructional supports and services consistent to support progress, and provides procedural safeguards to ensure that the plan is implemented and its effectiveness maintained.

6 Options for Service Delivery

The Individuals with Disabilities Education Act (IDEA), as amended in 1997 and 2004, places emphasis on the need to provide specialized instruction and services to students with disabilities in the least restrictive environment that allows the student to learn. For this reason, special education should be thought of as a service rather than as a place. Many models of service delivery exist because no one model meets the needs of all children, and IEP team members determine the location and types of service delivery that are most appropriate for a student. This chapter presents some of the program options, service delivery models, and strategies for school sites that are being used to assist students who have disabilities.

CONTINUUM OF PROGRAM OPTIONS

Each school district (local education agency), or consortium of districts or counties, is responsible for ensuring that a continuum of program options is available to assist students who have exceptional needs. Program options also include the related services that are necessary for supporting a student's educational progress. The usual options are listed as follows:

1. General education programs

2. Designated instruction and services

3. Resource programs

4. Special day classes

5. Alternative education

6. Nonpublic, nonsectarian schools or agencies

7. State special schools and centers

8. Home and hospital instruction

A student who is eligible for special education services may receive them through any one or a combination of the options that are the most appropriate for meeting the student's educational goals. The aim is always to deliver the service in the least restrictive environment in which the student can be assisted to function effectively. Those settings include educational, extracurricular, and nonacademic.

General Education Programs

General education programs are offered to all students in school without regard to any eligibility criteria. Students who have disabilities and who are in general education programs may be eligible for other programs, such as bilingual education, migrant education, or other programs that are designed to support students' educational achievements and to prevent students from dropping out of school. The practice of providing students with education in the least restrictive environment requires that special education and general education teachers work collaboratively to reduce the time that the student must be away from the general education classroom.

Special education students must have access to the general education curriculum and receive assistance to achieve the performance standards that are established for nondisabled students. A general education teacher must participate on the IEP team and assist in determining supplementary aids, services, and program modifications.

Designated Instruction and Services

Many students receive all their instruction in the general education classroom but also receive services by specially trained personnel. Related services include transportation and such developmental and corrective services as the following:

1. Speech-language pathology services

2. Audiology services

3. Interpreting services

4. Psychological services

5. Physical and occupational therapy

6. Recreation services, including therapeutic recreation

7. Social work services

8. School nurse services designated to enable a child with a disability to receive FAPE described in the child's IEP

9. Counseling services, including rehabilitative services

10. Orientation and mobility services

11. Medical services for diagnostic and evaluation purposes only

SOURCE: Adapted from Amendments to IDEA, 2004, Sec. 602(26)(A).

Resource Programs

Resource programs offer services to students who have disabilities and who are simultaneously enrolled in general education classes for the majority of the school day. Special education resource program teachers provide students and their parents with information, assistance, and materials; they can coordinate services and monitor student progress; and they participate in reviews and revisions of IEPs. Resource specialists must be fully qualified to perform the instructional activities that are permitted within the program, which includes subject matter competence in the areas in which they provide direct instruction.

Resource specialists often have wide latitude in the types of support that they can provide to reach the goals of an IEP. For instance, they can provide students with direct instruction in academic and performance areas to prepare students to succeed in instructional activities occurring in the general education classroom and instruct students who have disabilities within the general education classroom. They can collaborate with general education teachers in preparing instruction for students who have disabilities and they can also share their knowledge and experience during inservice training programs for teachers and parents.

At the secondary school level, the emphasis of the resource specialists' activities may change. While continuing to support students' progress in academic areas, the specialists may add career, vocational, and transitional instruction to assist a student prepare for postschool activities to their duties.

Special Day Classes

Sometimes a student's disability is so intense that even with supplementary aids and services, including curriculum modifications and behavioral support, he or she cannot achieve satisfactorily in the general education classroom for a majority of the school day. In such cases, the student is provided with instruction in special day classes that are located on the general school site. A student placed in settings outside the general education classroom must be able to participate in activities with nondisabled peers to the maximum extent appropriate. Such participation can consist of sharing classroom activities, meals, recess periods, elective classes, and extracurricular, recreational and other nonacademic activities.

The IEP team must document its rationale for placing a student in a program that is located outside the regular education. The documentation must indicate why the student's disability prevents appropriate learning in a less restrictive environment, in spite of special classroom interventions, such as accommodations, modifications, and supplementary aids and services.

Alternative Education

Alternative education programs in the context of IDEA are provided outside the regular or special school program and are interim placements for a child with a disability. This out-of-school placement is provided when a child violates a school code of conduct. Special education services are provided in these programs. Time limits and due-process safeguards govern procedures related to alternative placement.

Nonsectarian Schools or Agencies

Licensed nonpublic, nonsectarian school services are provided for children with disabilities whose needs cannot be met through the public school system. Students may be provided an education in a nonpublic, nonsectarian school setting at public expense if the placement is made by the IEP team. Assistance to children with disabilities in sectarian schools may also be provided.

State Special Schools and Diagnostic Centers

State special schools serve students for whom no appropriate placement is available in the special education local area. Special schools most commonly provide for students with severe visual impairment, severe hearing impairment, or severe multiple disabilities and who cannot be provided with an appropriate educational program in local schools.

States may also operate diagnostic centers that serve the state or a region of a state. The centers usually provide temporary residence for children who, because of their disabilities, need a level of educational diagnostic services that are not available in local public school settings. These centers can provide a continuum of assessment services that range from providing assessments at the student's school site or home to conducting multidisciplinary assessments at a diagnostic center's location. Assessments are designed to assist local IEP teams to determine appropriate curricula, instructional strategies, and program options for students. Diagnostic centers can also provide local educational agencies with a variety of training and staff development services for local school staff members who are involved in student programming issues.

SERVICE DELIVERY MODELS

A majority of students who have learning disabilities are assigned to regular classes and receive special instruction and assistance in a variety of ways. Resource specialists and other specialists, such as school psychologists and speech and language therapists, may see a child on a one-to-one basis, in small groups, or in one or more of the approaches that follow. Unique approaches are also tailored to meet unique situations.

Traditional Direct Service Model

In the context of the traditional direct service model, the resource specialist is responsible for conducting instructional assessments, assisting in the development of the IEP, and delivering special education services to students individually and in small groups in the resource room. The size of groups varies according to the severity of the disabilities of the students in the caseload. Effort is made to minimize disruption to the students' participation in core curriculum activities in the general education classroom. Students receive individualized instruction in strategies and skills that are necessary for learning the curriculum and for achieving grade-level standards. Frequency of service varies and must be stated on the IEP according to a student's needs.

Classroom Intervention: Co-Teaching Model

In the context of the classroom intervention–co-teaching model, the classroom teacher and the resource specialist provide instruction collaboratively. The following examples illustrate collaborative instructional activities: (a) the two teachers instruct side by side, (b) the resource specialist develops and models alternative teaching strategies for students who have learning disabilities in the general education classroom, and (c) the resource specialist provides the classroom teacher with modified materials, lesson plans, and tests. The resource specialist may also provide curriculum development, staff development, and parental training. This model is often chosen (a) when moving the student between two instructional settings could be disruptive, (b) when there is a sizable population that is at risk of academic failure in the general education classroom, and (c) when both teachers believe that a special student's needs can best be met within the general education classroom.

Consultative-Collaborative Model

The consultative-collaborative model is one in which the resource specialist advises, provides resources, answers questions, shares information, presents demonstrations, and assists in planning and reviewing the IEP with teachers, parents, administrators, and other support personnel. The resource specialist also provides instructional assessment services and advises staff on appropriate instructional programs and effective strategies for teaching students who have learning disabilities. The consultative-collaborative model differs from the classroom intervention model in that the general education teacher provides all the direct instruction to the student on the basis of the goals and objectives contained in an IEP.

Departmentalized Model for Students in Secondary Schools

In the context of the departmentalized model for students in secondary schools, the resource specialist usually teaches students who have exceptional needs during scheduled class periods. The curriculum may cover such academic content areas as reading, language, mathematics, and study skills, or it may concentrate on transition skills. The specialist teacher must be a fully qualified teacher under the provisions of federal and state law and entitled to provide instruction directly or under the direction of a qualified teacher in a manner prescribed by the state. Classes usually are scheduled for one period each day, five times a week. Students are scheduled into special education classes or resource programs as determined by the students' IEPs. Students receive course credit toward junior high school and senior high school graduation requirements.

STRATEGIES AND PROGRAMS FOR SCHOOL SITES

This section offers information about site-based strategies and programs that help create schools and programs that achieve high standards of performance, encourage the participation of all students and parents, and prepare students to function successfully after graduation. Strategies include schoolwide social support or buddy programs and peer problem-solving teams, service learning and community involvement; peer coaching; collaborative inservice training; schoolwide incentives; cross-age and peer tutoring; and articulation between school levels. Special education teachers need to participate fully in schoolwide and school-site improvement activities and to help shape the climate and culture of the settings in which they teach.

Schoolwide Strategies

In any general education classroom, teachers face great diversity in the language, culture, interests, skills, abilities, and needs of the students that they teach. Schools that effectively serve a diverse student population are committed to the belief that all students can and should succeed in the school's core academic curriculum and participate in extracurricular activities. Once the staff members, parents, administrators, and community members of a local school agree on and support this philosophy, it can become the foundation for action.

Schools that accept the challenge to promote universal success among their students develop schoolwide strategies that help them manage the different learning needs and improve the academic performances of all their students. The following options outline the kinds of school and community practices that are essential to achieving universal success:

1. The culture of the school celebrates individual and group growth and achievement in ways that recognizes differences in interests, abilities, and learning styles.

2. Students are provided with opportunities to learn so that they become fully involved and able to demonstrate their knowledge and skills.

3. The school's expectations for individualized performance take individual differences into account.

4. Varied learning environments are provided multiple rather than a single, standard mode of instruction.

5. Students are introduced to repertoires of learning strategies and study skills that emphasize reflective thought and systematic progress toward the goal of independent learning.

6. Students are encouraged and given incentives and opportunities to pursue academic and occupational goals, regardless of their native language, ethnic background, gender, or disability.

7. Students have opportunities to demonstrate their understanding through the use of authentic methods of assessment, such as the use of portfolios and projects.

8. Students can use technology to expand their access to information and to accommodate their differences.

9. Students have opportunities to participate in extracurricular and non-academic activities that recognize unique skills and foster competence and confidence.

Service Learning and Community Involvement

Service learning can be an effective adjunct to direct instruction. When working as volunteers in community services or projects, students have opportunities to improve the community, add meaning to classroom learning, broaden their knowledge and skills, participate in authentic learning experiences, apply multiple abilities, and achieve a sense of self-esteem. A well-constructed program provides effective community liaison; clear objectives and goals; active and meaningful participation; and opportunities to discuss, question, and analyze.

Through service learning, students who have learning disabilities gain an opportunity to experience success in valued activities that do not depend on academic skills or competition. Learning through helping can be a very positive experience for students who seldom have opportunities to demonstrate success in the classroom and therefore seldom receive legitimate recognition for jobs well done. Service learning can give students who have learning difficulties a chance to participate with equal skill in team efforts that result in a sense of personal value and community membership that is built on effort and results.

Peer Coaching

Peer coaching allows teachers to help each other improve their instructional effectiveness. The peer coaching model succeeds when teachers and their peer coaches work cooperatively. Training and release time are prerequisites to success. Peer coaching is most successful when teachers choose the coach with whom they prefer to work.

In this model the coach observes the teacher during an instructional activity. After the lesson, the coach and the teacher identify the intention of the lesson, the strengths of the lesson, and the most effective teaching techniques. The teacher is invited to discuss aspects of the lesson that could have been done differently or that did not go as well as expected with either a group of students or a particular student. The coach assists the teacher in identifying new teaching strategies for instructing students in the same content. The teacher then implements one of the new strategies in follow-up sessions and receives feedback from the coach.

Collaborative Inservice Training

Schools provide staff development sessions for their teachers and for other school personnel. Most school districts provide at least one inservice training day a year and other staff meetings devoted to professional growth. Educators who work in schools that participate in school-based coordinated programs have additional days allotted for professional development during which they may concentrate on acquiring the skills that they need to work effectively with students.

Special education teachers should participate with general education teachers in the staff development activities provided by the school unit. Most workshops are relevant to all teachers—imparting information about such areas as diagnostic teaching, learning styles, behavior management, and effective educational practices—and when general and special educators train together, they can share their expertise and compare different educational perspectives. Effective collaboration depends on the participation of skilled teachers who belong to a professional community and are a part of the school-site community.

Schoolwide Incentives

Schools in which all students succeed design programs that honor diversity in students' achievements. Such programs not only celebrate achievement but also recognize the efforts of students who have learning difficulties. For example, an elementary school that rewards students who read 1,000 pages by giving them membership in a Thousand Page Club can also reward students who achieve a significant increase in the number of pages that they read and can also make adjustments for levels of skill.

Schoolwide programs may honor students' achievements in areas other than academic subjects. Students who have learning difficulties may demonstrate strengths in the fine arts, athletics, service learning, community involvement, service to their families, cross-age tutoring, school attendance, and leadership. Recognition of students' achievements in these areas may help increase their feelings of self-worth and belonging to the school community—feelings that will increase their ability to tackle the difficult task of academic learning.

Cross-Age Tutoring and Peer Tutoring

In many classrooms, students are asked to help other students who are having academic difficulties. When students are in different grade levels, this helping activity is called *cross-age tutoring;* for example, a fifth-grade student tutoring a student in the first grade. When both students are in the same grade, this helping activity is called *peer tutoring*.

Cross-age tutoring and peer tutoring are beneficial when tutors have been trained in effective ways to prepare materials, give cues, and reinforce correct responses. If students practice tutoring through modeling and role-playing, training sessions can be completed in two or three half-hour sessions. In general, trained student tutors may help other students who have reading problems; the students who tutor definitely improve their own skills.

Articulation Between School Levels

Transitions between school levels—such as between preschool and elementary school, elementary school and middle school, middle school and high school, and high school and postgraduate activity—may be difficult for students and may break the continuity of instruction. These changes may be especially trying for students who have experienced difficulties in school.

Anticipating and planning for transitions may ease the disruption caused by moves between school levels. Visits to a new campus may reduce a student's uncertainties about what it is like to be there. Visits by students, teachers, or counselors from the receiving sites can provide human links that are important during transitions. Preplanned course schedules and extracurricular activities may reduce some of the mystery about the future.

In part, the break in the continuity of instruction between sites may be reduced by good communication between staff members from each site. Information from a student's report cards, cumulative files, and IEPs may assist receiving teachers in understanding a new student's skills and needs. Good course articulation and communication between teachers in similar subject fields can help improve the flow between subject levels.

Parents should be encouraged to maintain their own records of their child's history, progress, strengths, and achievements and of the accommodations that have worked effectively. Informed parents can be important advocates for their child and serve as allies to the teacher. Parents may often give the new teacher valuable information that has not yet arrived from the sending school. Parents may also gain insights about the ways in which they can best help their child through the transition and in the new classes. However, informed and confident students are often their own best advocates, especially in the upper grades. Teachers can help prepare students to become effective, reasonable, and tactful self-advocates.

Schoolwide Programs

This section describes site-based or schoolwide programs that are designed to improve overall school performance and individual student achievement. School reform and restructuring efforts take many forms.

Schoolwide efforts to improve a school's ranking among other schools or against a standard for improved achievement can have a serious impact on all the teachers in a school. Efforts to raise the achievement scores of children with disabilities in order to improve schoolwide scores or to prepare students for high school exit exams can lead to anxiety around test scores as well as to improvement in instructional practices.

School Restructuring

School reform and restructuring efforts are designed to meet the needs of an increasingly diverse population of students and parents and to manage the issues of students' outcomes. Changes are generally undertaken to affect the ways that students receive instruction or services and to increase the standards of performance. Administrators and instructional leaders are key participants in any attempt to change a school, but they need the encouragement and support of the staff and community to make lasting improvements. The principal helps staff members define the school's needs and recommend improvements in curriculum and instruction. These changes may involve new roles for a school's personnel, greater parental involvement, and an expanded use of community resources. Enriched subject matter offerings and varied instructional approaches may also be considered. Planning for such changes is crucial. Programs unique to a school's particular site may be developed to accelerate the achievements of students who perform below their potential. Special education specialists can play an important part in supporting a movement to achieve success for all students.

A Focus on Achievement Scores

A federal and state emphasis on individual and school achievement as measured by standardized tests set a direction in school reform that brings both challenges and blessings. Because the burden for improvement falls on the shoulders of teachers and administrators, the challenges for them are easy to see; the blessings are less apparent. This is especially true for conscientious professionals who work in schools located in high poverty areas and where there are many second-language-learners. Methods that adjust for these factors and credit growth may help restore the recognition for improvement. A few challenges and blessings are reported here.

Challenges

- Group tests do not take account of the growth toward individual goals and objectives.
- Schools may be punished because of low performance of students with disabilities.

- Teachers may be required to teach skills that have little to do with student needs.
- Test accommodations that could help students demonstrate true levels of achievement may not be allowed.

Blessings

- High expectations are introduced that may not have previously existed.
- Benchmarks for performance are provided for all students and therefore steps toward standards are also provided.
- The introduction of content previously avoided is encouraged, such as algebra and science.
- A focus on core curriculum is renewed, with periodic reporting and program adjustments.

SUMMARY

An IEP team is responsible for making decisions about a student's eligibility for special education, the student's educational plan, the delivery of services, changes in the goals, and the review of the student's progress. Once the information is before the IEP team, decisions can be made regarding goals, objectives, strategies, timelines, expected milestones, and the ways in which services will be delivered.

A student may be referred to a continuum of possible services; however, in most cases the student will be best served through a resource program that supports instruction in the general education classroom for the majority of the day. Many students will spend the entire instructional day in the general education classroom and receive designated instruction and services, such as speech therapy, which can be delivered in the general education classroom or in a separate room.

Attending a special day class is one of several options for students who cannot profit from spending the majority of their day in the general education classroom. An alternative education program is available on an interim basis for students with school code violations. Providing students who have disabilities with instruction through a nonpublic school or an agency is another option that IEP teams may choose to exercise.

Whichever service delivery model is selected, special education does not operate in a vacuum. Special education teachers are a part of a team of teachers at a school site. Each site is embedded in a community, and special education is a part of both the school and the surrounding community. Special education is influenced by the laws and initiatives that affect the school, and special education teachers should participate in school staff and district staff professional development opportunities. Contemporary movements in education have a direct effect on special education programs and demand the participation of special education professionals.

Afterword

As mentioned in the beginning, statements related to the law in *Addressing Learning Disabilities and Difficulties* have most often been adapted and distilled from the full legal text. We urge readers to review the original amendments and the related regulations of IDEA in order to make informed judgments or take appropriate action.

Readers who wish more information on specific learning disabilities are encouraged to read available professional literature, use the Internet resources available from professional organizations, contact their area's Parent Resource Center, or discuss the area of their interest with knowledgeable school or medical professionals. Some specific sources of additional information about the topics discussed in this book appear in the Resources and Selected References sections.

Glossary

Accommodation—An adaptation that does not fundamentally change a task, a test, or a course requirement

Adaptation—A change in instruction or assessment method that allows students to gain access to information and to demonstrate learning

Advocate—A person, parent, or professional who promotes the interests of students who have disabilities

Americans with Disabilities Act (ADA)—The Americans with Disabilities Act of 1990 extends civil rights protection to people who have disabilities The legislation covers employment, public accommodations, transportation, state and local government operations, and telecommunications

Antecedent—Anything that precedes or comes before a student's behavior; it can be adjusted to change the behavior

Aphasia—Impaired ability to acquire, understand, or articulate oral language due to damage to speech areas of the brain

Appropriate education—A legislated standard that is required by IDEA 1997; it guarantees that students who have disabilities will receive an educational program that is individually tailored to their abilities and needs

Assessment—The process by which information is gathered about students and evaluated to make educational decisions

Assistive technology—Any item, piece of equipment, or product that is used to increase, maintain, or improve the functional capabilities of persons who have disabilities

At-risk students—Students who because of their poor levels of achievement, their problematic behavior, or their social history are likely to drop out of school

Attention deficits—The characteristics of distractibility, inattention, and lack of focus often associated with learning disabilities that impair learning

Audiologist—A specialist who is trained in the evaluation of hearing and the detection of hearing loss

Auditory perception—The ability to perceive, decode, or encode auditory stimuli

Basic skills—The fundamental skills of listening, speaking, reading, writing, spelling, and doing arithmetic

Behavioral disorder—A condition of disruptive and inappropriate behavior that interferes with a student's learning and his or her relationships with others to such a degree that intervention is required

Behavioral goals and objectives—The expected and desired learning and behavioral outcomes for students that are based on planned interventions; the outcomes are stated in measurable terms so that the teaching and learning processes can be evaluated

Bilingual—The ability to speak—and possibly to read and to write—two languages, often with different levels of skill

Career education—A curriculum that is designed to teach the skills and the knowledge necessary in the world of work

Case manager—A person who is trained in making positive behavioral interventions and who helps plan and carry out an IEP-team-approved intervention or who supervises the person who carries out the intervention

Categorical program—Services provided by special funding and available only to a specific group of students; for example, low-income, under-achieving, gifted, disabled, English learner, or migrant students

Child finding—An effort required of school districts to locate and to identify children who have disabilities

Code of Federal Regulations (CFR)—Regulations developed by federal agencies to carry out the provisions of public laws; most special education regulations are found in Section 34 of the *CFR*

Collaboration—A group effort made by special education teachers, general education teachers, other service providers, and families who work together to provide effective services and education

Communicative disorders—An impaired ability to transmit or to receive information because of a speech disorder or language disorder

Consulting teacher—A specially trained teacher who serves as a resource person to advise and to provide instructional support to general education teachers who have students with disabilities

Cooperative learning—An instructional model in which students work together in teams to complete activities or assignments

Criterion-referenced test—An informal assessment strategy that measures the degree of a student's mastery of a subject

Culturally diverse students—Students who have an integrated pattern of behaviors based on beliefs, attitudes, actions, and learned and transmitted knowledge arising from their home and community

Decodable texts—Reading materials that provide an intermediate step between words in isolation and authentic literature; such texts are designed to give students an opportunity to learn to use their understanding of phonics in the course of reading connected text. Although decodable texts may contain sight words that have been previously taught, most words are wholly decodable on the basis of the letter-sound and spelling-sound correspondences taught and practiced in phonics lessons

Decoding—A series of strategies used selectively by readers to recognize and read written words; the reader locates cues (e.g., letter-sound correspondences) in a word that reveal enough about it to assist in pronouncing it and attaching meaning to it

Diagnosis—The process of identifying a person as having a disability by using tests, observations, and clinical judgment

Direct instruction—A method of teaching that is based on an understanding of the instructional needs of students and a systematic procedure for teaching, monitoring, evaluating, and providing practice

Disability—A physical, emotional, or cognitive condition that impairs a person's functioning

Discipline—Maintaining the order that is required to provide instruction to groups of students; discipline involves teaching self control, fostering appropriate conduct, and building cooperation among students

Dyscalculia—Impaired ability to perform math calculations or functions

Dysgraphia—Impaired ability to write

Dyslexia—A disorder manifested by the student's failure to attain the language skills of reading, writing, and spelling despite conventional instruction, the student's adequate intelligence, and sociocultural opportunity

English learner—A student, who through lack of experience, has a limited ability to comprehend, read, write, or speak English

Evaluation—An assessment or judgment of a student's characteristics, such as intelligence, physical abilities, sensory abilities, learning preferences, and achievement

Event recording—A method of recording observation data by which the number of times a behavior occurs is noted or the event is described

Exceptionalities—All the disabling conditions that may qualify a student to receive special education services

Explicit instruction—The intentional design and delivery of information by the teacher to the students; it begins with (a) the teacher's modeling or demonstration of the skill or strategy, (b) substantial structured opportunity for students to practice and apply newly taught skills and knowledge under the teacher's direction and guidance, and (c) an opportunity for feedback

Free appropriate public education (FAPE)—A legislated standard set forth in PL 94–142 and reaffirmed in subsequent amendments and regulations (i.e., Individuals with Disabilities Education Act 1997 and 2004); the standard guarantees that children who have disabilities are entitled to a free public education and the education plan and the special services necessary to meet individual educational needs

Functional behavior analysis—A form of assessment carried out by a trained professional to determine the nature of events surrounding a student's misbehavior and the antecedents and consequences of the behavior

Functional life skills—The skills that are needed to perform the everyday activities required in life

General education—The education that is designed to serve all students; it is also referred to as *regular education*

Graphic organizer—A visual tool to demonstrate the relationship between ideas, activities, or information

Guided practice—The performance of a task that is subject to supervision, encouragement, correction, and immediate feedback

Hyperactivity—Excessive activity that is bothersome or distracting to oneself or to others; it is characterized by a person's inability to sit or to concentrate for extended periods of time

Impulsivity—Abrupt action that is taken without a person's exercising careful thought or reflection; an impulsive person has problems with taking turns and organizing work

Inattention—A condition characterized by the failure to finish tasks that have been started, easy distractibility, a seeming lack of attention, and difficulty in concentrating on tasks that require sustained attention

Inclusion or full-inclusion programs—Educational programs in which students who have disabilities remain for a part or all of the day in the general education classrooms where they receive their specialized instruction and services

Independent practice—The student's performance of a skill without help or immediate supervision

Individualized education program (IEP)—A written plan of instruction and service that is required by the Individuals with Disabilities Education Act of 1997 and 2004 for every school-aged person who receives special education; the plan must include information about the child's current levels of educational performance, annual instructional goals, periodic evaluations, necessary accommodations, and related services. It must be prepared by an IEP team and reviewed annually

Individualized education program (IEP) team—An IEP team must include members specified in law, including parents and, when appropriate, the child; the team determines eligibility, develops an individualized education plan and evaluates and reviews progress and outcomes

Individualized instruction—Instruction that is designed to meet the individual needs of each child and that reflects specific objectives and goals

Individualized transition plan (ITP)—A section of the IEP that details the student's needs and services necessary for making the transition from school to postschool activities

Individuals with Disabilities Education Act, as Amended, 2004—The original legislation became law in 1975 and was referred to as the Education for All Handicapped Students Act (EHA). In 1986 it was renamed the Individuals with Disabilities Education Act. The Act is reauthorized every four years and ensures a free appropriate public education in the least restrictive environment for all infants, children, and youths who have disabilities

Instructional environment—The context in which instruction takes place, consisting of the social atmosphere, instructional strategies, classroom setting, books, materials, and equipment

Instructional goals—Annual goals written into the IEP concerning specific skills that the student needs to learn

Instructional objectives—Statements written into the IEP concerning the intermediate steps that a student is expected to achieve on his or her way to reaching an instructional or behavioral goal

Intellectual functioning—The actual performance of tasks that are believed to represent intelligence, such as observing, problem solving, and communicating

Interpreter—A person who speaks or signs the primary language of a parent or a child and who also speaks English; a person who can effectively translate communications between members of a school staff and a parent or a child

Learning differences—The variety of ways in which students learn or perform

Learning difficulty—A student's problem in achieving academic success on the basis of his or her ability to receive, process, or act on information

Learning disability—A specific learning disability is a disorder in one or more of the basic psychological processes involved in understanding or in using spoken or written language, and it may manifest itself in the imperfect ability to listen, think, speak, read, write, spell, or do mathematical calculation. The term, in law (IDEA, 2004), includes such conditions as perceptual disabilities, brain injury, minimum brain dysfunction, dyslexia, and developmental aphasia

Learning strategies—Instructional methods that assist students in attending, listening, reading, comprehending, and studying more effectively; methods that are usually designed to assist a student in acquiring, organizing, rehearsing, and recalling information

Least-restrictive environment—A major principle of IDEA that states that children who have disabilities should be included and should receive their education in a general education classroom along with their nondisabled peers; children with disabilities are also entitled to participate with nondisabled peers in nonacademic and extracurricular activities

Local educational agency (LEA)—Usually refers to a local school district but may refer to a group of districts or counties that operate or are funded as a unit

Mainstreaming—See *inclusion*

Manipulatives—Objects such as blocks or chips that can be used to represent a numeric quantity

Modalities—"The channels through which we perceive—visual, auditory, or tactile (touch)" (Harwell, 1989)

Modification—An adaptation that fundamentally changes a task, test, or course requirement

Morpheme—A linguistic unit of relatively stable meaning that cannot be divided into smaller meaningful parts; the smallest meaningful part of a word

Nondiscriminatory testing—Assessment or evaluation instruments or procedures that are not biased and that acknowledge differences in people's genders, cultures, or languages

Occupational therapist—A specialist who has received advanced training in the application of motor and coordination skills in everyday life and work

Orthography—The study of correct spelling according to established usage

Other health impaired—An eligibility category that is specified in IDEA 1997 that includes students who have limited strength, vitality, or alertness because of health problems; this category also includes students who have attention deficit disorders and attention deficit/hyperactivity disorders

Perceptual motor skills—The alignment or the integration of the ability to perceive and to understand information through the senses (visual, auditory, or tactile) with purposeful movement or motor activities (such as writing, speaking, or walking); see also *visual motor skills*

Peer tutor—A student who provides instructional assistance to another student; peer tutoring can be somewhat effective when the tutor is trained and monitored

Phoneme—The smallest unit of speech

Phonemic awareness—The insight that every spoken word is made up of a sequence of phonemes or speech sounds; this insight is essential for learning to read an alphabetic language because these elementary sounds or phonemes are represented by letters. Without phonemic awareness, phonics makes no sense; consequently, the spelling of words can be learned only by rote

Phonemic awareness instruction—Teaching awareness of words, syllables, and phonemes along a developmental continuum that spans rhyming, recognition and production, isolation, blending, matching of phonemes, segmentation, and substitution; early phonemic instruction should focus on exploration of the auditory and articulatory structure of spoken language, not on letter-sound correspondences

Phonics—A system of teaching reading and spelling that stresses basic symbol-sound relationships and their application in decoding words

Phonology—The rules of sounds of a language that combine to produce words, phrases, and sentences

Physical therapist—A specialist who has received advanced training in physical mobility and fluidity and who works with persons who have motor disabilities

Positive behavioral interventions—Strategies designed to improve a student's behavior and ability to learn by focusing on antecedent conditions and the function of misbehaviors and by supporting change in these areas

Program specialist—A school district employee who has expert knowledge about categorical programs and program options for students who have disabilities

Pullout activities—Activities during which students receive direct instruction, individually or in a small group, for a part of the school day in a special setting away from the general education classroom

Remediation—An instructional procedure that achieves improvement in a student's skills by correcting the errors or weaknesses in a student's performance

Resource specialist—A teacher who has received training in both regular education and special education and who works with students who have disabilities and who need special education services for a part of the school day

Resource specialist program—A special education service delivery model that provides service to the student for a part of the school day, either within or outside the general education classroom

Service learning—A program in the schools in which students volunteer, as a part of a class assignment, to work in charitable or community projects

Sight vocabulary/sight words—Words that are read automatically on sight because they are familiar to the reader

Special classes—Classes used exclusively for students who have special needs and who need intensive, specialized instruction generally for more than half of the school day

Speech, language, and hearing specialist—A specialist who has received advanced training in language development, articulation, and disorders of speech and language

Student success team (SST)—A process in general education through which selected members of the school staff meet to discuss students who are experiencing difficulties and to explore the ways in which the students' teachers or the school can improve the student's success

Systematic instruction—The strategic design and delivery of instruction that examines the nature of the objective to be learned and selects and sequences the essential skills, examples, and strategies necessary to achieve the objective by (a) allocating sufficient time to essential skills, (b) scheduling information to minimize confusion on the part of the learner, (c) introducing information in manageable and sequential units, (d) identifying prerequisite skills and building on prior knowledge of the learner, (e) reviewing previously taught skills, (f) strategically integrating old knowledge with new knowledge, and (g) progressing from skills in easier, manageable contexts to more complex contexts

Task analysis—The process of analyzing a task and breaking it into small, teachable subtasks

Test reliability—The degree to which a test is consistent and produces the same results on comparable forms of the test or at different times on the same test

Test validity—The degree to which a test measures what it claims to measure

Transition—A period of movement between school levels; for example, from preschool to kindergarten or from high school to the community; *transition* can also refer to the time between activities in a classroom

Visual motor skills—Refers to eye-hand coordination as it pertains to clarity or confusion between right or left and fine or gross motor movement; poor visual motor skills affect such skills as writing, drawing, running, kicking, throwing, or maneuvering the body. See also *perceptual motor skills*

Word attack (or word analysis)—Refers to the process used to decode words; students are taught multiple strategies to identify a word. This sequence progresses from decoding of individual letter-sound correspondences, letter combinations, phonics analysis and rules, and syllabication rules to analyzing structural elements (including prefixes, suffixes, and roots). Advanced word-analysis skills include strategies for identifying multisyllabic words

Resource A

*Characteristics and Criteria
for Identifying Students With
Learning Disabilities, Dyslexia,
Attentional Disorders, and
Behavioral Problems*

*T*his appendix provides an overview of learning disabilities, dyslexia, attention disorders, and behavioral problems that are encountered in general education classrooms that lead to a referral for assessment evaluation and that may qualify a child for special education services. Eligibility criteria for learning disabilities are currently undergoing revision as researchers continue to document the benefits of a "response-to-intervention" approach to eligibility as an alternative to the "discrepancy evaluation" approach which has traditionally been used. "Response-to-intervention" is explained in the section on learning disabilities.

The legislative definitions of specific learning disabilities grew out of study and research influenced by the fields of medicine, psychology, psychiatry, neurology, education, and special education. The definitions encompass an array of learning conditions and theories. They are not limited to a single skill or to a single cause of a disability but recognize a complex cluster of severe learning problems that may originate from single or multiple underlying causes.

Regardless of the different definitions and treatments of specific learning disabilities, the most common characteristic of all such disabilities is the significant difference that such students display between their age and grade levels and their levels of skill and performance in school. The discrepancy between the students' abilities and their performance is used to determine their eligibility to receive special education due to learning disabilities. However, there is disagreement among educators and school psychologists about the value of using the discrepancy model.

Federal laws and regulations have defined specific learning disabilities as follows:

> (i) General. The term means a disorder in one or more of the basic psychological processes involved in understanding or in using language, spoken or written, that may manifest itself in an imperfect ability to listen, think, speak, read, write, spell, or to do mathematical calculations, including conditions such as perceptual disabilities, brain injury, minimal brain dysfunction, dyslexia, and developmental aphasia.

> (ii) Disorders not included. The term does not include learning problems that are primarily the result of visual, hearing, or motor disabilities, of mental retardation, of emotional disturbance, or of environmental, cultural, or economic disadvantage (34 *CFR* 300.7[c] [10][i] and [ii]).

The federal definition is not a complete or perfect description, and it has competitors. For example, the National Joint Committee on Learning Disabilities (NJCLD, as quoted in Smith & Luckasson, 1992) has produced a more comprehensive definition of the nature of learning disabilities than is available in federal legislation, although it is not a legal definition:

> Learning disabilities is a general term that refers to a heterogeneous group of disorders manifested by significant difficulties in the acquisition and use of listening, speaking, reading, writing, reasoning or mathematical abilities. These disorders are intrinsic to the individual, presumed to be due to central nervous system dysfunction, and may occur across the life span. Problems in self-regulatory behaviors, social perception, and social interaction may exist with learning disabilities but do not by themselves constitute a learning disability. Although learning disabilities may occur concomitantly with other handicapping conditions (for example, sensory impairment, mental retardation, serious emotional disturbance) or with extrinsic influences (such as cultural differences or insufficient or inappropriate instruction), they are not the result of those conditions or influences. (p. 213)

Possibly the most important difference between the federal and the NJCLD definitions of learning disabilities is the committee's attention to the problem behaviors that are often associated with learning disabilities. These behaviors in themselves do not constitute a learning disability, but they occur frequently in connection with them. Whether there are common causes for academic problems and social problems or whether one problem contributes to the other is not clear. On the individual level, however, a relationship between academic and social problems often can be identified. For example, problem-solving difficulties in academic tasks may also be seen in problem-solving difficulties in social interactions.

Literature and research (Bender, 2001; Mercer & Mercer, 2001; Smith 2001) provide further clarity to the description of learning disabilities and the behavioral problems associated with them. Students who have learning disabilities often have difficulty transferring information from one setting or task to another, and their ability to generalize knowledge is limited. These students may be easily distracted and lack persistence on a task. Their language abilities, thinking abilities, and motor skills may be less than average for their age, and their motivation to work in school may be weak. Their social experiences are often less than satisfactory: Students who have learning disabilities often have a lower social status than their peers, are less accepted by their peers, and are less frequently selected in games. They interact less frequently and for shorter durations with peers and adults than do their grade mates. Their self-esteem in school is often low, and a sense of helplessness may prevail. In short, the possible interplay between academic problems and social problems is apparent.

Students who have learning disabilities may exhibit many of the academic and social problems just described, or they may have academic problems but few, if any, social problems. The constellation of problems for each student is different, so each student must be individually evaluated, and each special education program will be unique.

SPECIFIC LEARNING DISABILITIES

Terms used to identify learning disabilities are generally chosen to name the expressed condition or the presumed underlying cause of a condition. Such terms as *perceptual disabilities, brain injury,* and *minimal brain dysfunction* identify a physical cause for a disorder. Such terms as *dyslexia* (inability to read) and *aphasia* (inability to use words) describe the conditions themselves and derive from early Greek forms. The section that follows briefly explains the terms used in federal legislation to identify specific learning disabilities.

Perceptual Disabilities

Perceptual disabilities appeared to be a likely culprit early in the search for the cause of learning disabilities. The common reversals of the letters *b* and *d* or *p* and *g* and confusion around words that look alike suggested that problems with perception might be at the root of learning problems. This observation, linked with observations of the poor physical coordination that is often present in students who have learning disabilities, led to a movement that assumed a perceptual-motor basis for learning disabilities. Some educators in the early years of special education subscribed to this point of view and developed teaching strategies based on it.

Subsequent research studies have not been kind to the perceptual-motor theory of learning disabilities. Although the theory recognizes the complex process that builds the eye-hand coordination that underlies a student's ability to copy or to replicate through movement what he or she sees, the application of the theory has not been widely successful in helping students who have learning disabilities, though some of the findings have been useful in physical education and in improving some students' eye-hand movement skills.

Brain Injury and Minimal Brain Dysfunction

The brain and the central nervous system are at the center of the process that we call learning. Clear evidence exists to show that brain injury can interrupt, damage, or impede learning, and it can interfere with speech, thinking, and movement. As early as 1919, Kurt Goldstein, a renowned neuropsychologist working with men who had war-related brain injuries, discovered that these people experienced severe learning problems and hyperactivity. Research continues to explore the links between brain function and various aspects of thought, memory, perception, feeling, and learning.

Known brain injury in students is rare, but when a student's learning is impaired because of a brain injury, the student is eligible for assistance under the learning-disability category of federal legislation. The current methods of intervention borrow from existing methods and have not been organized into separate procedures.

The term *minimal brain dysfunction* is a reference in IDEA '97 to a suspected central nervous system problem that is not detectable through standard neurological examinations. Some educators have proposed that minimal brain dysfunction may be the possible cause of perceptual-motor problems and other forms of learning disabilities. However, as with other brain-related theories and research, what is understood about minimal brain dysfunction has not added significantly to the instructional practices used in working with students who have learning disabilities. In fact, the existence of minimal brain dysfunction is not strongly supported by clinical research and has not resulted in educational applications.

Dyslexia

Overview

Historically, the term *dyslexia* applied to severe difficulty in learning to read despite generally good instruction and intelligence. Learning to read is a complex process, however, and involves the coming together of auditory, sensory, motor, language, and cognitive skills. A disturbance in any or all of those areas can impact learning. Thus dyslexia has come to encompass a variety of disruptions and symptoms around language-based learning and performance.

In 1878 a German doctor, Adolph Kussmaul, identified a patient with what he called "reading blindness." Eight years later, Rudolph Berlin, another German doctor, in describing a similar patient coined the word "dyslexia." In the 1920s in the United States, Dr. Samuel Orton, a neurologist, studied children with reading problems and used the term *dyslexia* to identify their condition. Orton focused on a multisensory approach to improve reading instruction, and Anna Gilligham's application of her knowledge of the structure of language to Orton's procedures resulted in the Orton-Gilligham Method of instruction. That method, with variations, permeates the methods used by a number of reading programs today.

Examples of authors with current variations on the Orton-Gilligham Method are listed as follows. These methods generally have in common the use of a multisensory (seeing, hearing, and touching) approach to instruction. They use structured language and active learner participation. This is not an all-inclusive list, nor is it intended to be an endorsement of a specific method.

Alphabetic Phonics

Barton Reading and Spelling System

Herman Method

Multisensory Teaching Approach (MTA)

Slingerland

Wilson Reading System

Recipe for Reading

Effects of Dyslexia

The effect of reading disabilities on children should not be underestimated. Reading is a basic skill that supports much of classroom instruction and most of the independent academic learning that occurs in school today. The inability to read denies youth and adults access to written information vital to success in school and in postschool employment. At the same time that children with reading problems struggle to improve, good readers learn new skills, such as text understanding, advanced writing, and problem solving. Advanced related skills might never be adequately taught to poor readers because the classroom time devoted to these subjects passes while the child struggles with lower skills.

Children with dyslexia may also have poor verbal expressive skills, including problems with language structure, vocabulary, and fluency. Written skills in spelling and writing often lag behind reading skills, compounding classroom failure. These difficulties can be the result of the disorder or the lack of successful, adequate, or timely school experience.

The impact of school failure on a child's sense of adequacy and self-confidence can be alarming and long lasting. Many children, without help, pass into adulthood bearing the remnants of the failure that they experience in school. For instance, as adults they might feel they cannot read, long after their skill has improved. They might self-select jobs below their ability because they lack confidence based on years of school failure.

Early identification and attention to reading difficulties can improve children's chances to succeed in school and in later life. The contributions of Orton, Gilligham, and others who followed have significantly improved the reading instruction of children with dyslexia.

Definitions

It is easy to become confused about the terms *dyslexia* and *learning disabilities*. The term *dyslexia* was born out of the work of neurologists and continues to have a strong link to neurology. Learning disabilities, on the other hand, are more educationally based, and reading disabilities are viewed from an education perspective. The definition of dyslexia often includes the disabilities of writing, spelling, language, and arithmetic. A definition of learning disabilities, however, often includes an umbrella of specific learning disabilities, such as reading, writing, spelling, cognition, language, and arithmetic. It might not include the term *dyslexia*. Both address the issue of poor reading.

The definition of dyslexia adopted by the board of directors of the International Dyslexia Association on November 12, 2002 (www.interdys .org), states the following:

Dyslexia is a specific learning disability that is neurological in origin. It is characterized by difficulties with accurate and/or fluent word recognition and by poor spelling and decoding abilities. These difficulties typically result from a deficit in the phonological component of language that is often unexpected in relation to other cognitive abilities and the provision of effective classroom instruction.

Secondary consequences may include problems in reading comprehension and reduced reading experiences that can impede the growth of vocabulary and background knowledge.

National Institute of Neurological Disorders and Stroke (www.ninds .nih.gov) provides statements for both dyslexia and learning disabilities:

> **Dyslexia** is a brain-based type of learning disability that specifically impairs a person's ability to read. These individuals typically read at levels significantly lower than expected despite having normal intelligence. Although the disorder varies from person to person, common characteristics among people with dyslexia are difficulty with phonological processing (the manipulation of sounds) and/or rapid visual-verbal responding.
>
> **Learning disabilities** are disorders that affect the ability to understand or use spoken or written language, do mathematical calculations, coordinate movements, or direct attention. Although learning disabilities occur in very young children, the disorders are usually not recognized until the child reaches school age.

The American Psychiatric Association, in its publication *Diagnostic and Statistical Manual of Mental Disorders*, Fourth Edition (*DSM-IV*), does not refer to "dyslexia." The *DSM-IV*, however, does describe "reading disorder," "math disorder," and "disorder of written expression." These disorders are described within a section on learning disorders that is included in a larger section titled "Disorders Usually First Diagnosed in Infancy, Childhood, or Adolescence."

The Learning Disability Association of America (www.ldanatl.org) identifies dyslexia as involving reading and related language-based learning disabilities, and IDEA (www.nectac.org/idea/105-17partc.asp) lists it along with other disabilities under specific learning disabilities.

The confusion around the term dyslexia is the result of disagreement and inconsistencies among professionals on the definition of dyslexia and the accuracy and/or appropriateness of current neurological knowledge about the origin of the disability and treatment options.

Evaluation for Dyslexia

It is important to have a child evaluated when the child exhibits signs of a reading or language problem. These problems might appear in oral understanding or expression and in reading, writing, or spelling. Math understanding and computation might also be involved. To establish the presence of dyslexia, other causative factors need to be eliminated, such as inadequate instruction, sensory or motor impairment, adverse environmental conditions, or low intelligence. In young children poor motivation can follow successive failure; it is seldom an initial cause of failure.

A child should not be subjected to persistent failure in any skill or endeavor. The old adage "Success breeds success" is true with children. The opposite is also true: "Failure breeds failure." Therefore, whenever a child is unsuccessful with a task or a skill, it is necessary to determine the source of the problem and provide assistance. Persistent problems require professional help. Early detection and help are almost always justified because in most cases early attention and intervention can forestall future problems or at least reduce negative effects.

Schools can usually provide evaluation personnel, and, failing this, professionals outside the school can be located through friends, health providers, parent resource centers, and other community resources. If the child is found to be eligible for special education assistance, the rights of the child and the parent are protected under the Individuals with Disabilities Act and subsequent amendments. Evaluation involves the assessment of areas of performance affected and background and developmental information. Possible physical causes need to be eliminated.

Characteristics

Dyslexia is characterized by characteristics a persistent problem in learning to read, write, and spell and can include significant problems in one or more of the following areas:

Speaking

Listening

Memorizing

Computing

Recalling

Note taking

Organizing

Strategies for Improvement

Because dyslexia is resistant to ordinary classroom instruction, specialized instruction and accommodations are required. These can be accomplished in the standard classroom by an accomplished teacher, but the student's needs often exceed available classroom time and might require individual or small-group instruction.

The following are a few of many strategies that can help children with dyslexia succeed in school:

- Provide multisensory and structured instruction in reading.
- Use strategies of instruction and provide strategies for learning that assist the student organize, remember, and apply skills and knowledge.
- Provide extra time to complete assignments and multiple ways to access written knowledge (e.g., books on tape, videotapes, class discussions, personal readers, tutors).
- Assist the student develop strategies that improve attending and listening skills.
- Assist child to understand how his or her difficulty impacts on the child's personal performance and help the child discover personal ways to accommodate or compensate for problem(s) until it is (are) corrected.
- Use alternative ways to evaluation students so that the child's true level of understanding or performance can be measured.

Summary

Children with dyslexia can be helped by early identification and instruction targeted to individual children's needs. These children suffer personal frustration and often can frustrate their parents and teachers. Seldom can teachers or parents, working alone, provide the help that is needed. Schools often have the specialized staff that can provide effective interventions. If it is not forthcoming, however, the parent needs to seek assistance outside the school. Both parents and teachers need to be strong advocates for these children because special efforts are required to improve their chances for success. Eventually these children need the maturity, knowledge, and skill to become self-advocates.

Developmental Aphasia

Developmental aphasia is a disorder in learning and in using spoken or oral language. This condition is considered a learning disability, except that it falls more often within the purview of the large and long-standing profession of language, speech, and hearing specialists. Aphasia is one of many speech and language disabilities that involve problems with articulation, auditory skills, and voice. The speech and language disciplines have professionals credentialed to provide special education services who may also assist general classroom teachers in providing developmental language instruction. Special classes are sometimes provided for the more seriously disabled aphasic students and are taught by teachers from backgrounds in language, speech, and hearing or in learning disabilities, depending on each state's policies. Other professionals licensed by the state provide services in clinics, hospitals, or private practice.

Aphasia as a disability will not be discussed further in this document and was included only to provide a perspective on the breadth of learning disabilities. In the larger context of students who have difficulty in learning from conventional instruction, students with aphasia have complex problems with learning language. Persons wishing to learn more about this disability should consult their local language, speech, and hearing specialist or special education director.

ATTENTIONAL DISORDERS

Attentional disorders are included in federal legislation under the category of "other health impairment." According to the federal definition,

> Other health impairment means having limited strength, vitality or alertness, including a heightened alertness to environmental stimuli, that results in limited alertness with respect to the educational environment, that—
>
> (i) Is due to chronic or acute health problems such as asthma, attention deficit disorder or attention deficit hyperactivity disorder, diabetes, epilepsy, a heart condition, hemophilia, lead poisoning, leukemia, nephritis, rheumatic fever, and sickle cell anemia; and
>
> (ii) Adversely affects a child's educational performance. (34 *CFR* 300.7[c][9][i] and [ii])

Attention Deficit Disorder and Attention-Deficit/Hyperactivity Disorder

Students who have attention deficit disorder (ADD) or attention-deficit/hyperactivity disorder (ADHD) exhibit a severe degree of inattentive, hyperactive, impulsive, or disruptive behaviors that affect their ability to learn and to function effectively. A discussion about these disorders is provided in this handbook because ADD and ADHD are frequently associated with learning disabilities and with academic difficulties. In addition, the instructional strategies used with students who have ADD and ADHD are consistent with the strategies used with students who have learning disabilities. Likewise, the behavioral strategies used with students who exhibit inappropriate behaviors are similar to those used with students who have ADHD. The next two sections offer a medical definition of ADHD, a description of its characteristics, and some strategies for managing and improving the behavior of students who have ADHD. (Please note that variations in the way that attentional disorders are identified in this handbook occur because federal regulations refer to both ADD and ADHD, but the medical reference cited refers to ADHD only.)

A Definition of ADHD

A medical definition of ADHD is provided in the *Diagnostic and Statistical Manual of Mental Disorders* (American Psychiatric Association, 2000). The manual provides a narrative description of attention-deficit/hyperactivity disorder that contains information on diagnostic features; subtypes; recording procedures; associated features and disorders; specific culture, age, and gender features of the disorder; its prevalence, course, and familial patterns; and criteria for making a differential diagnosis. The manual also recognizes three subtypes of ADHD: Combined Type, Predominantly Inattentive Type, and Predominantly Hyperactive-Impulsive Type.

Diagnostic Criteria for Attention-Deficit/Hyperactivity Disorder

A. Either (1) or (2):

   (1) six (or more) of the following symptoms of **inattention** have persisted for at least 6 months to a degree that is maladaptive and inconsistent with developmental level:

Inattention

   (a) often fails to give close attention to details or makes careless mistakes in schoolwork, work, or other activities
   (b) often has difficulty sustaining attention in tasks or play activities
   (c) often does not seem to listen when spoken to directly
   (d) often does not follow through on instructions and fails to finish schoolwork, chores, or duties in the workplace (not due to oppositional behavior or failure to understand instructions)
   (e) often has difficulty organizing tasks and activities
   (f) often avoids, dislikes, or is reluctant to engage in tasks that require sustained mental effort (such as schoolwork or homework)
   (g) often loses things necessary for tasks or activities (e.g., toys, school assignments, pencils, books, or tools)
   (h) is often easily distracted by extraneous stimuli
   (i) is often forgetful in daily activities

(2) six (or more) of the following symptoms of **hyperactivity-impulsivity** have persisted for at least 6 months to a degree that is maladaptive and inconsistent with developmental level:

Hyperactivity
    (a) often fidgets with hands or feet or squirms in seat
    (b) often leaves seat in classroom or in other situations in which remaining seated is expected
    (c) often runs about or climbs excessively in situations in which it is inappropriate (in adolescents or adults, may be limited to subjective feelings of restlessness)
    (d) often has difficulty playing or engaging in leisure activities quietly
    (e) is often "on the go" or often acts as if "driven by a motor"
    (f) often talks excessively

Impulsivity
    (g) often blurts out answers before questions have been completed
    (h) often has difficulty awaiting turn
    (i) often interrupts or intrudes on others (e.g., butts into conversations or games)

B. Some hyperactive-impulsive or inattentive symptoms that caused impairment were present before age 7 years.

C. Some impairment from the symptoms is present in two or more settings (e.g., at school [or work] and at home).

D. There must be clear evidence of clinically significant impairment in social, academic, or occupational functioning.

E. The symptoms do not occur exclusively during the course of a Pervasive Developmental Disorder, Schizophrenia, or other Psychotic Disorder and are not better accounted for by another mental disorder (e.g., Mood Disorder, Anxiety Disorder, Dissociative Disorder, or a Personality Disorder).

SOURCE: Reprinted with permission from the *Diagnostic and Statistical Manual of Mental Disorders,* Copyright 2000. American Psychiatric Association.

Characteristics of Attention-Deficit/Hyperactivity Disorder

A 1993 edition of the journal *Exceptional Children,* titled "Special Issue: Issues in the Education of Children with Attention Deficit Disorder" provides a comprehensive discussion on the significance of ADHD in education.

This issue and particularly the article by Sydney Zentall, "Research on the Educational Implications of Attention Deficit Hyperactivity Disorder," provide valuable information on the subject.

Students who have ADHD may have difficulty

1. Listening selectively to a message while ignoring background auditory stimulation or competing information.

2. Attending to a basic message that involves detail or lacks explanations. The student prefers global cues ("it looks like") to detail ("it has these parts").

3. Responding to a question that is unaccompanied by external cues, such as pictures or other visuals. The student can become talkative, however, when he or she initiates a conversation.

4. Comprehending long reading passages, even when having an adequate vocabulary.

5. Reading, in part because of other disabilities the student may have, such as dyslexia.

6. Computing, because of problems in handling multiple operations, organizing verbal information, eliminating extraneous information, and being attentive to repetition.

7. Maintaining clear handwriting during lengthy classroom assignments, especially copying.

Teachers consistently mention that their greatest need for professional development is in the area of behavior management. Students who are demanding, disruptive, impulsive, aggressive, bossy, outspoken, or hyperactive are a challenge and a distraction to teaching. When students' poor basic skills and low achievement are combined with serious behavior problems, teachers face a dual challenge—how to teach and how to manage behavior.

One approach for managing students who have ADHD is the use of medication to reduce hyperactivity and depression and to increase a student's ability to pay attention. However, even when a student is taking medication, the teacher often needs to use skillful behavioral support to help the student profit from classroom instruction. The accommodations and instructional strategies described in this publication can help students who have ADHD achieve academically. In addition, the teacher can often help parents and physicians by monitoring a student's behavioral and academic processes in school, noting changes in the student's behavior, and reporting those changes to the parent and, with the parent's approval, to the student's physician.

BEHAVIORAL PROBLEMS

As noted earlier, behavioral problems in themselves do not constitute a learning disability, per se; however, they frequently occur in connection with learning disabilities. Effective classroom and individual management strategies are designed to create an orderly, safe, and focused environment in which to learn; to enhance cooperative, collaborative, and competitive activities among learners; and to develop individual self-management skills. Attention to both group and individual management strategies can help establish and maintain a classroom environment in which energy is focused on learning.

SUMMARY

Students who have learning disabilities often exhibit a constellation of learning, attentional, and behavioral difficulties. A disability can affect one or more academic and cognitive areas and both academic achievement and social behavior. Learning disabilities can be reduced, corrected, or avoided through appropriate instruction and support.

Fear of violence in the schools decreases tolerance for behavioral problems and increases the chances that students who have learning disabilities, attentional disorders, and behavioral problems will be removed from school. Strategies to support positive behaviors are a critical element of a program that works toward the students' academic success and behavioral improvement. A program that is designed to improve both levels of achievement and behavior can have the most beneficial and lasting effect on students' growth.

Resource B

Selected Internet Sites

U sing the Internet is an efficient method for locating current information on specific subjects related to learning difficulties and learning disabilities. Nearly all publishers and book distributors maintain an Internet home page that will lead to an index of their inventories. Most organizations also have an Internet home page that links to many other useful Internet sites. In addition, an Internet search can be tailored to answer a specific question. This appendix lists the addresses and brief descriptions for Internet sites that may provide readers with the latest information, research, and activities in the fields of learning difficulties and learning disabilities.

All Kinds of Minds
    http://www.allkindsofminds.org
    A network of parents and professionals in support of Dr. Mel Levine's neurodevelopmental model to understand learning differences and learning difficulties

Alliance for Technology Access
    http://www.ataccess.org/
    A network of parents and professions dedicated to increasing the use of technology by children and adults with disabilities

American Institutes for Research
    http://www.air.org
    Serves as a source of research projects and reports in areas of education, including assessment and special education

Ask Jeeves for Kids
    http://www.ajkids.com
    Supplies answers to students' questions on an extremely wide variety of topics; also offers advice, help, and information on a selection of topics

Center for Applied Special Technology
http://www.cast.org
Provides information on the ways in which technology can be used to improve the success of persons who have disabilities; discusses the application of universal design for learning

Center for Effective Collaboration and Practice
http://www.air.org/cecp
Promotes services for children and youths who have behavioral and emotional problems

Council for Exceptional Children
http://www.cec.sped.org
International organization of parents and professionals in special education; provides timely information on NCLB and IDEA 2004

Dr. Mac's Amazing Behavior Management Advice Site
http://maxweber.hunter.cuny.edu/pub/
Provides a bulletin board on which to post a detailed description of a student's behavior problem; advisors provide written comments and suggestions

Education World
http://www.educationworld.com
Provides information on current education topics, including academic subjects, educator's needs, and support issues

Family and Advocates Partnership for Education
http://www.fape.org
Informs families and advocates about the 1997 Individuals with Disabilities Education Act

Federal Resources for Educational Excellence
http://www.ed.gov/free
Provides education resources especially useful to teachers and organized by school subject areas

IDEA Practices
http://www.cec.sped.org
Supports the implementation of the Individuals with Disabilities Education Act; provides extensive coverage of educational issues, resources, and links to other related Internet sites

LD Online

http://www.ldonline.org

Provides comprehensive online information and resources related to learning disabilities

The Library of Congress

http://www.loc.gov

Features information that can be fun and useful to teachers, parents, children, and youths

National Center for the Dissemination of Disability Research (NCDDR)

http://www.ncddr.org

Makes research information available about youths and adults with disabilities

National Center on Educational Outcomes

http://education.umn.edu/nceo/

Publishes online information about graduation requirements, state standards, and state assessments of students who have disabilities

National Center to Improve the Tools of Educators

http://idea.uoregon.edu/~ncite

Features online technical reports that provide a synthesis of research on relevant educational topics; describes current programs and projects pertaining to persons who have disabilities; provides links to special and general education Internet sites

National Dropout Prevention Center/Network

http://www.dropoutprevention.org

Offers resources to support staff who work to improve the success of schools in preventing early exits from secondary schools

The National Information Center for Children and Youth with Disabilities

http://nichcy.org

Provides comprehensive information and links to other Internet sites related to the needs of families, educators, and other professionals who interact with children and youths who have disabilities

National Institute for Literacy

http://novel.nifl.gov

Promotes the creation of a fully literate nation; provides resource listings and links to related Internet sites

National Institute for Urban School Improvement

http://www.edc.org/urban

Links education reform networks with special education networks; specializes in urban issues and contains pages for a library, an electronic newsletter, other publications, an urban forum, and information about events

Nonverbal Learning Disabilities Online

http://www.nld.com

Provides a wealth of information about research, organizations, resources, and conferences having to do with nonverbal learning disabilities

Schwablearning: A Parent's Guide to Helping Kids with Learning Difficulties

http://www.schwablearning.org/

Timely articles and links to a variety of resources, monthly newsletter

Special Education Resources on the Internet

http://seriweb.com/

Provides links to many Internet sites related to children who have disabilities

Technical Assistance Alliance for Parent Centers

http://www.taalliance.org

Offers technical assistance for parent training and information projects; contains Internet Web site links to parent training centers and resources across the United States

Technical Assistance Center on Positive Behavioral Interventions and Supports

http://pbis.org

Supports the use of positive behavioral interventions and supports in families, schools, and communities; contains related fact sheets, research briefs, case studies, and PowerPoint presentations

Wrightslaw: Advocacy and Legal Resources for Parents

http://www.wrightslaw.com/

Up-to-date information on special education law and advocacy

Resource C

Agencies and Organizations

This resource provides information about public agencies; national foundations, centers, and parent organizations; and state and national professional organizations through which help may be obtained for persons who have learning disabilities and their families.

Public Agencies

National Information Center
for Children and Youth
with Disabilities
PO Box 1492
Washington, DC 20013-1492
(800) 695-0285
http://www.nichcy.org

National Institute of
Child Health and
Human Development
Building 31, Room 2A32
31 Center Drive
Bethesda, MD 20892
(301) 496-5133
http://www.nichd.nih.gov

U.S. Department
of Education
400 Maryland Avenue SW
Washington, DC 20202-0498
(800) 872-5327
http://www.ed.gov

U.S. Department of Education
Education Resource
Organization Directory
330 C Street SW
Washington, DC 20202
(800) 421-3481
http://www.ed.gov/Programs/bastmp

U.S. Department of Education
Office for Civil Rights
330 C Street SW
Washington, DC 20202
(800) 421-3481
http://www.ed.gov/about/offices/list/
ocr/index.html

U.S. Department of Education
Office of Special Education and
Rehabilitative Services
330 C Street SW
Washington, DC 20202
(800) 421-3481
http://www.ed.gov/about/offices/list/
osers/index.html

National Foundations, Centers, and Parent Organizations

The Charles Schwab Foundation
for Learning
1650 South Amphlett Boulevard,
Suite 300
San Mateo, CA 94402
(800) 230-0988
http://www.schwablearning.org

National Center for Learning Disabilities
318 Park Avenue South, Suite 1401
New York, NY 10016
(888) 575-7373
http://www.ncld.org

Parent Advocacy Coalition
for Educational Rights
PACER Center
8161 Normandale Boulevard
Minneapolis, MN 55437-1044
(952) 838-9000
http://www.pacer.org

National Professional Organizations

American Speech-Language-Hearing
Association
10801 Rockville Pike
Rockville, MD 20852
(800) 638-8255
http://www.asha.org

Children with Attention Deficit Disorders
(CHADD)
8181 Professional Place, Suite 201
Landover, MD 20785
(800) 233-4050
http://www.chadd.org

Council for Exceptional Children
1110 North Glebe Road, Suite 300
Arlington, VA 22201-5704
(888) 232-7733
http://www.cec.sped.org

Council for Learning Disabilities
PO Box 40303
Overland Park, KS 66204
(913) 492-8755
http://www.cldinternational.org

International Dyslexia Association
Chester Building, Suite 382
8600 La Salle Road
Baltimore, MD 21286-2044
(410) 296-0232
http://www.interdys.org

Learning Disabilities Association
of America
4156 Library Road
Pittsburgh, PA 15234-1349
(412) 341-1515
http://www.ldanatl.org

National Association of School
Psychologists (NASP)
4340 East West Highway, Suite 402
Bethesda, MD 20814
(301) 657-0270
http://www.nasponline.org

National Attention Deficit Disorder
Association (ADDA)
1788 Second Street, Suite 200
Highland Park, IL 60035
(847) 432-ADDA
http://www.add.org

Nonverbal Learning Disabilities
Association
2446 Albany Avenue
West Hartford, CT 06117
(860) 570-0217
http://www.nlda.org

Selected References

The number of research, conceptual, and program articles in the field of learning difficulties and learning disabilities increases dramatically every year as does the number of textbooks and published materials. The following list provides a variety of sources and a sample of research articles and thought on relevant topics and also includes the sources cited in the text.

Accommodation

California Department of Education, Special Education Division. (1999). *A parent's guide to achievement testing.* Sacramento: Author. Retrieved from http://www.cde.ca.gov/spbranch/sed/prntgui.pdf

Hollenbeck, K., Tindal, G., & Almond, P. (1998). Teachers' knowledge of accommodations as a validity issue in high-stakes testing, *Journal of Special Education, 32*(31), 175–183.

IDEA Partnerships. (2000). *Making assessment accommodations: A toolkit for educators.* Reston, VA: Council for Exceptional Children.

Kame'enui, E. J., & Carnine, D. W. (1998). *Effective teaching strategies that accommodate diverse learners.* Upper Saddle River, NJ: Prentice-Hall.

Assessment—Functional

Daly, E. J., III, Witt, J., Martin, B., & Dool, E. (1997). A model for conducting a functional analysis of academic performance problems. *School Psychology Review, 26*(4), 554–574.

Gable, R. (Ed.). (1999). Conducting functional behavioral assessment: New roles and new responsibilities (entire issue). *Preventing School Failure, 43*(4), 167–170.

O'Neill, R. E., Horner, R., Albin, R., Storey, K., & Sprague, J. (1997). *Functional assessment and program development for problem behavior* (2nd ed.). Pacific Grove, CA: Brooks/Cole.

Assessment—General

California Department of Education, Special Education Division. (1999). *Guidelines for individual evaluation of California students with disabilities, birth through age twenty-one.* Sacramento: Author. Retrieved from http://www.cde.ca.gov/spbranch/sed/evalguid.htm

Green, J. F. (1993, November). *Psycholinguistic assessment: Critical components in identifying dyslexia.* Paper presented at the 44th International Conference of the Orton Dyslexia Society, New Orleans, LA.

Heumann, J. E. (2000). Questions and answers about provisions in the Individuals with Disabilities Education Act Amendments of 1997 related to students with disabilities and state and district-wide assessments (Memorandum 00-24). Washington, DC: Office of Special Education Programs.

Jones, E. D., Southern, W., & Brigham, F. J. (1998). Curriculum-based assessment: Testing what is taught and teaching what is tested. *Intervention in School and Clinic, 33*(4), 239–249.

Shinn, M. (Ed.). (1998). *Advanced applications of curriculum-based measurement.* New York: Guilford.

Torgesen, J. K., & Wagner, R. K. (1998). Alternative diagnostic approaches for specific developmental reading disabilities. *Learning Disabilities Research and Practice, 13*(4), 220–232.

Behavior—General

Buck, G. H., Polloway, E., Kirkpatrick, M., Patton, J., & McConnell, K. (2000). Developing behavioral intervention plans: A sequential approach. *Intervention in School and Clinic, 36*(1), 3–9.

Emmer, E. T., & Stough, L. M. (2001). Classroom management: A critical part of educational psychology, with implications for teacher education. *Educational Psychologist, 36*(2), 103–112.

Rademacher, J. A., Callahan, K., & Pederson-Seelye., V. A. (1998). How do your classroom rules measure up? Guidelines for developing an effective rule management routine. *Intervention in School and Clinic, 33*(5), 284–289.

Wright, D. B., & Gurman, H. B. (2001). *Positive intervention for serious behavior problems: Best practices in implementing the Hughes Bill (Assembly Bill 2586) and the positive behavioral intervention regulations* (Rev. ed.). Sacramento: California Department of Education.

Behavior—Social

Elksnin, L. K., & Elksnin, N. (1998). Teaching social skills to students with learning and behavior problems. *Intervention in School and Clinic, 33*(3), 131–140.

Forness, S. R., Sweeney, D. P., & Wagner, S. (1998). Learning strategies and social skills Training for students with AD/HD. *Reaching Today's Youth, 2*(2), 41–43.

Gresham, F. M., Sugai, G., & Horner, R. (2001). Interpreting outcomes of social skills training for students with high-incidence disabilities. *Exceptional Children, 67*(3), 331–344.

Characteristics

American Psychiatric Association. (2000). *Diagnostic and statistical manual of mental disorders* (4th ed., text rev.). Washington, DC: Author.

Bender, W. N. (2001). *Learning disabilities: Characteristics, identification, and teaching strategies* (4th ed.). Needham Heights, MA: Allyn & Bacon.

Fuchs, L. S., & Fuchs, D. (1998). Treatment validity: A unifying concept for reconceptualizing the identification of learning disabilities. *Learning Disabilities Research and Practice, 13*(4), 204–219.

Smith, D. D. (2001). *Introduction to special education: Teaching in an age of opportunity* (4th ed.). Needham Heights, MA: Allyn & Bacon.

Smith, D. D., & Luckasson, R. (1992). *Instructor's annotated edition for introduction to special education: Teaching in an age of challenge.* Needham Heights, MA: Allyn & Bacon.

Vaughn, S., Linan-Thompson, S., & Hickman, P. (2003). Response to instruction as a means of identifying students with reading/learning disabilities. *Exceptional Children, 69*(4), 391–409.

Zentall, S. S. (1993). Research on the educational implications of attention deficit hyperactivity disorder. *Exceptional Children, 60*(2), 143–153.

Instruction—General

California Department of Education. (1997). *Guidelines for language, academic, and special education services required for limited-English-proficient students in California public schools, K–12.* Sacramento: Author.

California Department of Education. (1999). *Service-learning: Linking classrooms and communities.* Sacramento: Author.

Fulk, B. M, & Stormont-Spurgin, M. (1995). Fourteen spelling strategies for students with learning disabilities. *Intervention in School and Clinic, 11,* 16–20.

Harwell, J. M. (1989). *Complete learning disabilities handbook: Ready-to-use techniques for teaching learning-handicapped students.* West Nyack, NY: Center for Applied Research in Education.

Mercer, C. D., & Mercer, A. R. (2001). *Teaching students with learning problems* (6th ed.). Upper Saddle River, NJ: Prentice Hall.

Morocco, C. (Ed.). (2001). Teaching for understanding with students with disabilities: New directions for research on access to the general education curriculum [Special Issue]. *Learning Disability Quarterly, 24*(1).

Ormsbee, C. K., & Finson, K. D. (2000). Modifying science activities and materials to enhance instruction for students with learning and behavioral problems. *Intervention in School and Clinic, 36*(1), 10–21.

Instruction—Reading

California Department of Education. (1999). *Reading/language arts framework for California public schools, kindergarten through grade twelve.* Sacramento: Author.

Curtis, M. E., & Longo, A. M. (1999). *When adolescents can't read: Methods and materials that work* (Vol. 1). Cambridge, MA: Brookline.

Mastropieri, M. A., & Scruggs. T. E. (1997). Best practices in promoting reading comprehension in students with learning disabilities: 1976 to 1996. *Remedial and Special Education, 18*(4), 197–213.

Moore, D. W., Alvermann, D. E., & Hinchman, K. A. (2000). *Struggling adolescent readers: A collection of teaching strategies.* Newark, DE: International Reading Association.

Law

California Department of Education. (2000). *Special education rights of parents and children under the Individuals with Disabilities Education Act, Part B.* Sacramento: Author.

California Education Code § 56337 (n.d.). Retrieved from http://caselaw.lp.findlaw.com/cacodes/edc/56333-56338.html

Code of Federal Regulations, Title 34, § 300 (2000).

Freedman, M. K. (2000). *Testing, grading and granting diplomas to special education students: Individuals with Disabilities Education Law Report—Special report no. 18.* Horsham, PA: LRP.

Individuals with Disabilities Education Act. (2004). Retrieved from http://www.ed.gov/offices/OSERS/IDEA

Student Success Teams

Bahr, M. W., Whitten, E., Dieker, L., Kocarek, C., & Manson, D. (1999). A comparison of school-based intervention teams: Implications for educational and legal reform. *Exceptional Children, 66*(1), 67–83.

Bullock, L. M., & Menendez, A. L. (2001). Meeting the needs of children and youth with challenging behaviors; Module 17: The role of student support teams in meeting the needs of children and youth with challenging behaviors. *Reaching Today's Youth, 5*(2), 46–52.

Radius, M., & Lesniak, P. (1997). *Student success teams: Supporting teachers in general education.* Sacramento: California Department of Education.

SST Student Success Teams. (2000). Santa Cruz: California Dropout Prevention Network.

Transition

California Department of Education. (2001). *Transition to adult living: A guide for secondary education.* Sacramento: Author.

DeFur, S. H. (1999). *Transition planning: A team effort* (Transition Summary 10). Washington, DC: National Information Center for Children and Youth with Disabilities.

Geenen, S., Powers, L., & Lopez-Vasquez, L. (2001). Multicultural aspects of parent involvement in transition planning. *Exceptional Children, 67*(2), 265–282.

Index

Page references followed by *t* indicate a table; followed by *fig* indicate an illustrated figure.

individualized, 129
Orton-Gilligham Method of
    Instruction, 139
phonemic awareness, 131–132
phonics, 32, 132
remediation procedure during, 132
systematic, 133
Instruction strategies
    to improve mathematical
        computations/operations,
        16, 27–31t
    to improve mathematical
        reasoning/problem solving,
        29–32, 33t–34t
    to improve performance skills,
        41–65
    to improving learning, 16–40
Instructional environment, 129
Instructional goals, 130
Instructional objectives, 130
Intellectual functioning, 130
International Dyslexia Association, 140
Interpreter, 130
Intervention plans
    for learning improvement
        strategies, 40
    for performance improvement
        strategies, 66
    See also Teachers
ITP (individualized transition plan), 129

Jamie's story, 41
Jason's story, 29, 49
Jon's story, 54

Kussmaul, A., 139

Language issues
    aphasia as, 3, 125, 143–144
    auditory perception as, 126
    bilingual abilities as, 126
    dyslexia as, 2, 3, 127
    during evaluation process, 79–80
    interpreter to aid with foreign, 130
    native language definition as, 79–80
    See also Communication;
        Verbal expression
LEA (local educational agency), 130
Learning
    assumptions about, 4
    community service, 116, 132
    cooperative, 127
    "getting ready to learn" skill for, 15

identification of strengths/weaknesses
    in student, 5
observation to recognize
    ineffective, 2–3
Learning abilities approach, 2, 5
Learning differences, 130
Learning difficulties
    approaches to children's, 5–6
    background on, 1–3
    basic assumptions regarding, 4
    benefits of addressing, 7–8
    complexity of, 3–4
    defining, 130
    early identification of, 4
    using handbook to address, 6
    limitations of addressing, 8–9
Learning disabilities
    ADD (attention deficit disorder),
        3, 144–147
    ADHD (attention deficit/hyperactivity
        disorder), 3, 144–147
    behavioral problems associated with,
        137, 148
    brain injury and minimal brain
        dysfunction and, 138
    developmental aphasia, 3, 125, 143–144
    efforts to identify children with, 126
    federal regulations defining specific,
        87–89, 136–137
    lack of consensus regarding, 2
    National Institute of Neurological
        Disorders and Stroke
        definition of, 141
    NJCLD definitions of, 136–137
    perceptual disabilities, 137–138
    terms used to describe, 3
    See also Disability; Dyslexia
Learning disability approach, 5
Learning Disability Association of
    America, 141
Learning disabled, 5
Learning disordered, 5
Learning improvement strategies
    for ability to pay attention,
        17, 19–20, 21t–22t
    intervention plan used with, 40
    for listening comprehension,
        16–17, 18t
    for mathematical computations/
        operations, 16, 27–29, 30t–31t
    for mathematical reasoning/problem
        solving, 29–32, 33t–34t
    for productivity, 16, 25, 27, 28t

CORWIN PRESS